SYDNEY

in a Week

Wendy Moore

SYDNEY
in a Week

NH
NEW
HOLLAND

CONTENTS

Introduction   10

Exploring Sydney

Day One – Birthplace of Sydney   12

Day Two – Heart of the City   28

Day Three – Darling Harbour and Chinatown   44

Day Four – Bondi and the Eastern Suburbs   58

Day Five – Manly and the Northern Beaches   72

Day Six – Exploring the Western Harbour   86

Day Seven – West to the Blue Mountains   100

Special Itineraries

A Day at the Zoo   114

Harbourside Walks   120

Bushwalking in the Royal National Park   126

Cruising Sydney's Waterways   132

Central Coast Getaway   138

Winelover's Tour of the Hunter Valley   144

Southern Highlands   150

South Coast   156

Directories

Shopping   *164*

Cuisine   *166*

Nightlife   *168*

Events   *170*

Index   174

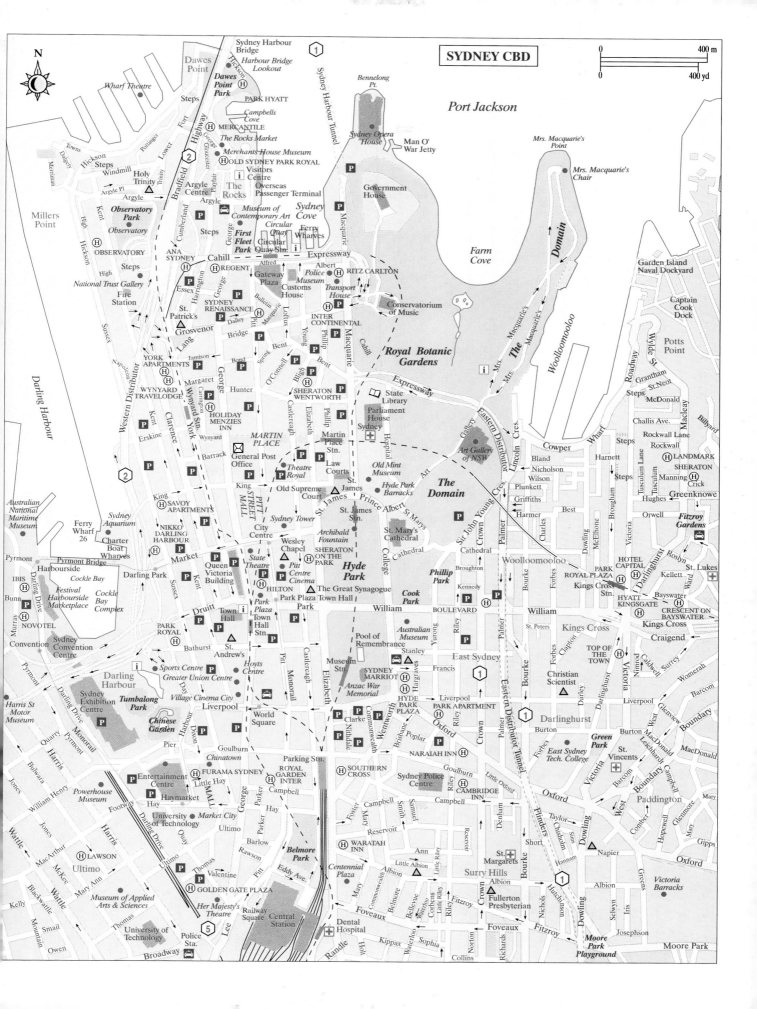

SYDNEY CBD

0 — 400 m
0 — 400 yd

Port Jackson

N

Dawes Point

Sydney Harbour Bridge
Harbour Bridge Lookout
Wharf Theatre
Dawes Point Park
PARK HYATT
Campbells Cove
MERCANTILE
The Rocks Market
Merchants House Museum
OLD SYDNEY PARK ROYAL
Visitors Centre
Overseas Passenger Terminal
Holy Trinity
Observatory Park
Observatory
OBSERVATORY
National Trust Gallery
Fire Station
ANA SYDNEY
REGENT
Museum of Contemporary Art
First Fleet Park
Circular Quay Stn.
Ferry Wharves
Circular Quay
Sydney Cove
Sydney Opera House
Man O' War Jetty
Mrs. Macquarie's Point
Mrs. Macquarie's Chair
Bennelong Pt.
Government House
Farm Cove
The Domain
Garden Island Naval Dockyard
Captain Cook Dock
Potts Point

Millers Point
Hickson Steps
Windmill
Argyle Pl
Argyle
High
Kent
Steps
Essex
SYDNEY RENAISSANCE
St. Patrick's
Grosvenor
YORK APARTMENTS
WYNYARD TRAVELODGE
HOLIDAY MENZIES INN
SAVOY APARTMENTS
NIKKO DARLING HARBOUR
Bradfield Highway
Lower Fort
George
Gloucester
Cumberland
Harrington
Argyle Centre
ARGYLE
Steps
Cahill
Alfred
Gateway Plaza
Customs House
Police Museum
RITZ CARLTON
Transport House
INTER CONTINENTAL
Conservatorium of Music
Royal Botanic Gardens
Albert
Macquarie

Darling Harbour
Napoleon
Sussex
Kent
Clarence
York
Erskine
Barrack
Wynyard
MARTIN PLACE
General Post Office
Theatre Royal
Law Courts
Old Supreme Court
St. James
King
PITT STREET MALL
City Centre
Sydney Tower
State Theatre
Queen Victoria Building
Town Hall
St. Andrew's
Jamison
Margaret
Hunter
O'Connell
Bent
Spring
Phillip
Bligh
SHERATON WENTWORTH
Martin Place Stn.
St. James Stn.
Prince Albert
Hyde Park Barracks
Old Mint Museum
Archibald Fountain
St. Mary's Cathedral
Cook Park
Phillip Park
Carrington
Bond
Bridge
Pitt
Castlereagh
Elizabeth
Macquarie
Young
Loftus
Phillip
Bent
Cahill Expressway
State Library
Parliament House Sydney
Hospital
Art Gallery of NSW
The Domain
Lincoln Cres.
Cowper
Bland
Nicholson
Wilson
Griffiths
Harmer
Best
Charles
Crown
Palmer
Bourke
Forbes
Kennedy
Broughton
Phillip Park
Woolloomooloo
HOTEL CAPITAL
PARK ROYAL PLAZA
Kings Cross Stn.
HYATT KINGSGATE
Cathedral
St Marys
College
St. Mary's Cathedral
Hyde Park
SHERATON ON THE PARK
Wesley Chapel
Pitt Centre Cinema
The Great Synagogue
Park Plaza
Town Hall Stn.
HILTON
Park Plaza
William
BOULEVARD
Riley
Yurong
Stanley
Australian Museum
Pool of Remembrance
Museum Stn.
SYDNEY MARRIOT
Anzac War Memorial
HYDE PARK PLAZA
PARK APARTMENT
East Sydney
Francis
Liverpool
NARAIAH INN
Crown
Palmer
Bourke
St. Peters
Forbes
Clapton
Burton
Forbes
Kings Cross
Craigend
TOP OF THE TOWN
Christian Scientist
CRESCENT ON BAYSWATER
Kings Cross
Darlinghurst
Victoria
Darley
Liverpool
Green Park
St. Vincents
East Sydney Tech. College
MacDonald
Burton
Leichhardt
Campbell
Bayswater
Kellett
St. Lukes
Roslyn
Ward
Grantham
St. Neot
McDonald
Challis Ave.
Rockwall Lane
Rockwall
Tusculum Lane
Tusculum
Manning
Crick
Greenknowe
Hughes
Orwell
Fitzroy Gardens
LANDMARK SHERATON
Wylde St.
Macleay
Billyard
Roadway

Australian National Maritime Museum
Pyrmont
Ferry Wharf 26
Sydney Aquarium
Charter Boat Wharves
Pyrmont Bridge
Harbourside
Cockle Bay
IBIS
Festival Harbourside Marketplace
Cockle Bay Complex
NOVOTEL
Convention
Sydney Convention Centre
Darling Harbour
Sports Centre
Greater Union Centre
Hoyts Centre
Village Cinema City
Liverpool
World Square
Museum Stn.
Harris St Motor Museum
Sydney Exhibition Centre
Tumbalong Park
Chinese Garden
Powerhouse Museum
Entertainment Centre
Haymarket
FURAMA SYDNEY
Little Hay
Chinatown
ROYAL GARDEN INTER
Parking Stn.
SOUTHERN CROSS
Sydney Police Centre
CAMBRIDGE INN
University of Technology
Market City
Belmore Park
WARATAH INN
Centennial Plaza
Surry Hills
St. Margarets
Fullerton Presbyterian
Museum of Applied Arts & Sciences
LAWSON
Ultimo
Her Majesty's Theatre
GOLDEN GATE PLAZA
University of Technology
Police Sta.
Broadway
Railway Square
Central Station
Dental Hospital
Moore Park Playground
Moore Park
Victoria Barracks
Paddington
Oxford

Darling Harbour
Darling Park
Darling Park
PARK ROYAL
St. Andrew's
Bathurst
Druitt
Market
Kent
Sussex
Monorail
Castlereagh
Pitt
Liverpool
Goulburn
Dixon
Hay
Pier
Harbour
Quay
Ultimo
Thomas
Valentine
Barlow
Rawson
Pitt
Eddy Ave.
Lee

Millers Point
Harris
Quarry
Bulwara
William Henry
Jones
MacArthur
McKee
Mary Ann
Blackwattle
Kelly
Owen
Smail
Mountain
Wattle
Footway
Harris
Pyrmont
Jones
Thomas

East Sydney
Bourke
Crown
Riley
Commonwealth
Wentworth
Clarke
Nithdale
Brisbane
Poplar
Oxford
Goulburn
Campbell
Foster
Mary
Smith
Samuel
Reservoir
Ann
Little Albion
Albion
Foveaux
Commonwealth
Belmore
Bellevue
Fitzroy
Crown
Bourke
Waterloo
Sophia
Kippax
Holt
Randle
Collins
Little Riley
Corbens
Albion
Nichols
Hutchison
Dowling
Fitzroy
Foveaux
Denham
Short
Hannam
Bourke
Reservoir
Campbell
Little Oxford
Oxford
Flinders
Taylor
Sims
Chisholm
Napier
West
Comber
Glenmore
Hopewell
Mary
Gipps
Oxford
Greens
Iris
Selwyn
Josephson
Victoria Barracks

Eastern Distributor Tunnel
Sir John Young Cres.
Eastern Distributor
Mrs. Macquarie's
The Domain

NEW
HOLLAND

Published in Australia by
New Holland Publishers (Australia) Pty Ltd
Sydney • Auckland • London • Cape Town
14 Aquatic Drive Frenchs Forest NSW 2086 Australia
218 Lake Road Northcote Auckland New Zealand
24 Nutford Place London W1H 6DQ United Kingdom
80 McKenzie Street Cape Town 8001 South Africa

First published in 1997
Second edition published in 1999
Revised and updated edition published in 2000

Copyright © 1997 in text: Wendy Moore
Copyright © 1997 in captions: Steve Elias
Copyright © 1997 in photographs: photographers as credited below
Copyright © 1997 in maps: New Holland Publishers (Australia) Pty Ltd
Copyright © 1997 New Holland Publishers (Australia) Pty Ltd

National Library of Australia Cataloguing-in-Publication Data:

Moore, Wendy.
Sydney in a week: the ultimate guide to Sydney.

Rev. and updated ed.
Includes index.
ISBN 1 86436 675 3.

1. Sydney (N.S.W.)—Guidebooks. I. Title.

919.4410466

Publishing General Manager: Jane Hazell
Publisher: Averill Chase
Editors: Joanne Holliman, Laurence Lemmon-Warde
Designer: Laurence Lemmon-Warde
Cartographers: Mark Seabrook, James Mills-Hicks
Picture researchers: Karen Adler, Bronwyn Rennex

Reproduction by cmyk prepress
Printed and bound in Malaysia by Times Offset (M) Sdn Bnd

HALF-TITLE PAGE *Arriving in Sydney need not be so bumpy, but the city does hold many surprises.*
TITLE PAGE *Rocky headlands fold in and protect a number of Sydney's beaches and its harbour.*
CONTENTS PAGE *Sydney lights up at night, sending neon colours across its famous waterways.*
CBD MAP PAGE *The jewel of the harbour is undoubtedly the Sydney Opera House.*
IMPRINT PAGE *A glorious sunset frames the city and casts its colour upon the harbour.*
INTRODUCTION PAGE *Boats of all sizes leave their white wakes on the blue waters of Sydney Harbour.*

PHOTOGRAPHIC CREDITS
Copyright © in photographs **NHIL** (Shaen Adey) with the exception of the following:
Bill Green: p6, 21; **Arne Falkenmire:** p112; **Stuart Gaut:** p140; **NHIL** (Vicki Hastrich): p131; **Heidi Herbert:** p138;
Geoff Higgins: p15 (top left), 27, 93; **Paul Steel:** pp12–13; **Dave Watts:** p115; **NHIL:** pp30; 66, 109 (bottom), 133 (inset), 135 (top and bottom), 137 (top);
NHIL (Anthony Johnson): cover (inset), pp1, 3, 6, 8, 29 (inset), 32–33, 36, 42 (top), 45 (inset), 51 (top), 62–63; 79 (bottom), 81 (top left), 114–115,
118 (top left), 165 (top), 167 (bottom); **NHIL** (Nick Rains): cover (spine), pp2, 5, 18 (top, and bottom right), 22 (far left), 37 (bottom), 39 (top),
43, 46, 47, 53 (bottom), 55 (top), 56, 65 (left), 70 (bottom), 80, 81 (top right and bottom), 92 (bottom), 97, 98 (top and bottom), 99, 100–101,
101 (inset), 102, 103, 107, 111 (bottom), 113, 124 (top), 139, 141, 142 (top and bottom), 143, 147 (bottom), 148 (far left), 148 (right centre), 150,
153 (top, and bottom right), 154 (bottom), 156, 162, 165 (bottom), 172 (bottom right); **photolibrary.com:** p16-17, 36, 48-49, 56 (top)
compliments of **State Transit, Sydney Discovery Tours:** p60 (top); compliments of **Taronga Zoo:** pp117 (bottom), 119.
NHIL = New Holland Image Library

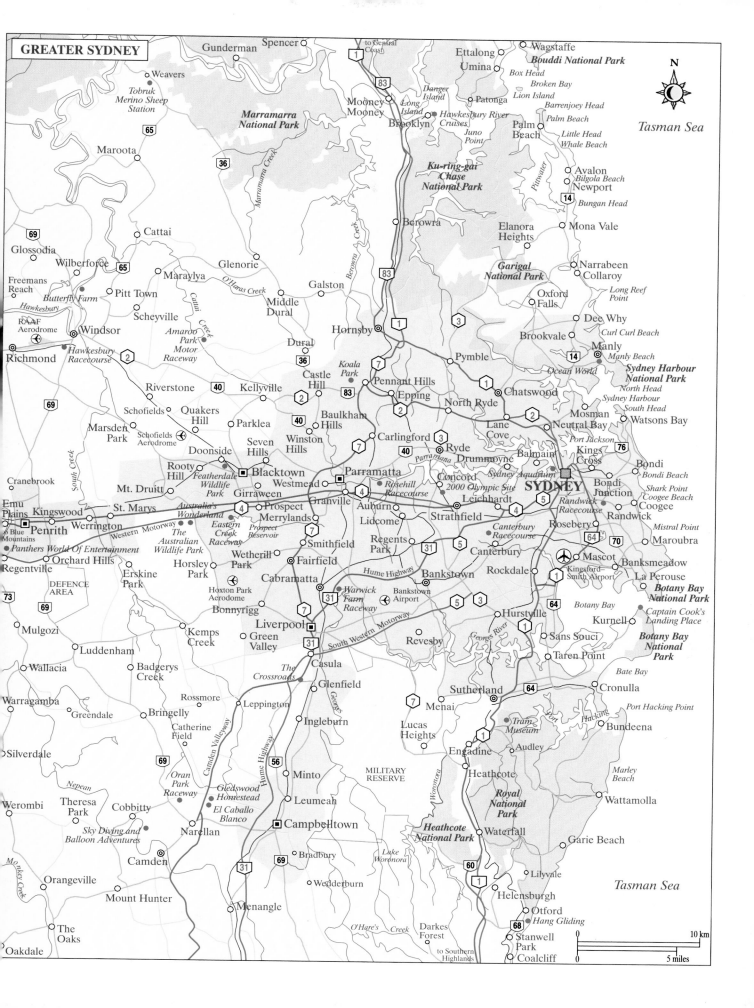

$\mathcal{S}$ydney, capital of New South Wales, is without a doubt, one of the world's most beautiful cities. The harbour, the Opera House, the Harbour Bridge and the spectacular beaches are images known throughout the world. The pleasure of actually seeing and being in this wonderful city can never really be expressed in words, and there is never enough time to explore and sample all the city has to offer. SYDNEY IN A WEEK has been specially written to help you make the most of your time with seven comprehensive day tours, eight special itineraries and a number of convenient directories provided.

Each day tour begins at Circular Quay, the ferry and ra terminal on Sydney Cove, and covers a different section o the city. We've given you a number of transport options t suit your fitness and time schedule. For example, eac walking tour also gives directions for bus transport. All th tours can be accomplished in a day, however, many of yo may be tempted to stop and spend more time at one c the sights along the way. Art lovers may well wish to spen the afternoon at the gallery, history buffs at the Hyde Pai Barracks, while families with children may like to visit th dinosaur exhibitions at the Australian Museum.

All of the special itinerary trips are within a two-hour drive of the city centre. They would be best accomplished by car but we've provided alternative bus or train options. Check with your hotel, local travel agent or tourist information centre for any special tours or packages that may also be available. If you have a little more time, many of these trips would make fabulous weekend or overnight stays.

The directories will guide you to some of Sydney's best dining and shopping venues, plus let you know which pubs to visit, where to catch a stage show, experience the ballet or see a movie, or how to find the city's many exciting nightclubs.

And as a bonus there is a calendar of the major events that happen throughout the city and its surrounding areas.

I've really enjoyed gathering all the information for this book and in the process I've rediscovered why I love this city so much. No matter how long you've got – a day, a week, a month – or whether you are visiting on holiday or on business, you'll never be able to see everything that this gem of a city has to offer. But SYDNEY IN A WEEK will help you to quickly sort through the huge maze of information and decide what you want to see, when and how.

Wendy Moore

Birthplace
of Sydney

Day One

BIRTHPLACE OF SYDNEY

Circular Quay • The Rocks • Sydney Harbour Bridge • Sydney Observatory
Argyle Place • Sydney Opera House • Mrs Macquarie's Chair • Royal Botanic Gardens
Museum of Sydney • Harbour Twilight Cruise

Ever since 1788, when Captain Arthur Phillip and the 11 ships of the First Fleet sailed into Sydney Harbour and began European settlement of Australia, **Sydney Cove** has been the city's focal point. It is fitting, then, that this first tour should start at **Circular Quay**, the ferry and rail terminal at the head of the cove. The day's schedule can easily be accomplished by walking, and it encompasses all the sights located around the city's dominant symbols, the monumental Sydney Harbour Bridge and the Sydney Opera House, and includes the historic district known as The Rocks to the west of Sydney Cove, the Royal Botanic Gardens around **Farm Cove** to the east, and a number of prominent buildings and museums.

From humble beginnings

Enclosing the promontory and shoreline west and north of Circular Quay is **The Rocks**, the colony's original urban settlement. The inhabitants at that time were the convicts who built the wharves, roads and residences of the late-18th and early-19th centuries when Sydney's most affluent building spree took place under the governorship of Lachlan Macquarie. The Rocks was also a notorious thieves' kitchen during those days when sails ruled the seas, and ocean-going clippers were the only contact the colony had with the outside world. This old urban quarter is now a splendidly restored enclave of historical sandstone houses, waterfront cafes, restaurants, pubs, galleries and tourist shops.

PREVIOUS PAGES *Sydney Opera House and Harbour Bridge provide a grand entrance to what must be the world's most beautiful harbour.*

INSET *The restored warehouses of Campbells Storehouse on Sydney Cove are a marvellous place to eat, drink and soak up the atmosphere.*

ABOVE *The hub of the harbour is Circular Quay, where ferries and ocean liners dock within the protected waters of Sydney Cove.*

ABOVE LEFT *The sleek RiverCat, arriving at Circular Quay from its run along the Parramatta River, is just one of Sydney's many passenger ferries.*

ABOVE RIGHT *First Fleet Park is an excellent place to enjoy a picnic and watch the ferries on the harbour before continuing with the day's sightseeing.*

BELOW *The Museum of Contemporary Art offers a cross-section of international modern art including masterpieces such as Roy Liechtenstein's* Crying Girl.

Begin by walking west from the Quay around the harbour. You'll pass the open, grassy **First Fleet Park**, where urbanites escape on sunny lunch hours and busking musicians, magicians and acrobats ply their trade along the promenade. Here you can take some time to appreciate the wonderful panorama of ferries coming and going on the sparkling harbour between those two dual Australian icons, the Sydney Harbour Bridge and the Sydney Opera House.

Museum of Contemporary Art – from offices to art

The sandstone, 1930s Art Deco building to your left is the **Museum of Contemporary Art**. This building originally served as the offices of the Maritime Services Board, which controls harbour shipping. The museum was opened in 1991 and exhibits a wide range of Australian and international contemporary artists. The works include an interesting collection of film, laser, television, photography, sculpture and painting mediums, and often a fusion of the forms. The museum's **MCA Cafe** (*see* Cuisine) is renowned for its current Sydney-style cuisine, espressos and pastries; it would make a wonderful place to stop for morning tea.

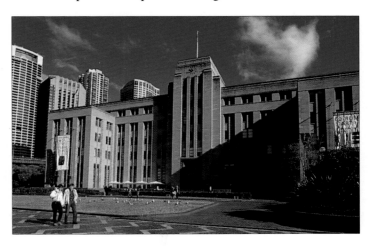

Birthplace of Sydney

Kings Cross

Royal Botanic Gardens

Farm Cove

Circular Quay

Sydney Opera House

Sydney Cove

Sydney Harbour B

Port Jackson

Kirribilli

Bradfield Highway

Milsons Point

Sydney Tower

Darling Harbour

The Rocks

Wharf Theatre

Pier One

Lavender Bay

George Street – the oldest thoroughfare

Continuing around West Circular Quay, behind the **Overseas Passenger Terminal** where ocean liners, navy boats and cruise ships are often docked, are stairs which lead to George Street. At the top is the Sailor's Home, built in 1864, which is now **The Rocks Visitor Centre** and the meeting place for guided tours of the district.

On the left is **Cadman's Cottage**, a whitewashed house looking like a misplaced Irish country cottage. Built in 1815 it is the city's oldest surviving residence and now houses the information office of the National Parks Shop. John Cadman, the house's original owner, was a pardoned convict who became the harbour superintendent.

George Street, Australia's oldest thoroughfare, once hosted many of the almost 50 taverns which contributed to The Rocks' bawdy seaport reputation.

Walking north along George Street you pass the **Mariners' Church** (1856) and a collection of superb 19th-century shopfronts that feature Dutch gable roofs and pyramidal towers, where the company scouts of the colonial shipping offices used to

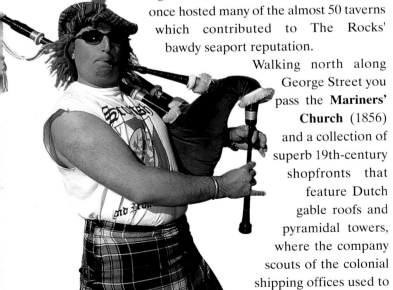

look out to the Heads through their telescopes to keep score of the ships that were coming into the harbour.

On weekends the north end of George Street is covered with a number of canopies and becomes a market boasting over 140 stalls selling a wide variety of products (*see* Shopping). To the right, just as you enter Hickson Road is a set of stairs beside the sawtooth-roofed Campbell Storehouse (1861) which leads to Campbells Cove. The warehouses are now popular waterfront restaurants with outdoor seating offering the most superb harbour panoramas. Moored in the cove, where clippers and schooners from all over the known world once docked is the replica of the HMAS *Bounty*, built for the film *Mutiny on the Bounty* starring the Australian actor Mel Gibson. The original ship, captained by the unfortunate Captain Bligh, who later became a governor of the colony, was torched by Fletcher Christian and his mutineers at Pitcairn Island in 1789. The replica ship sails from The Rocks daily on lunch and dinner cruises around the harbour, its inlets and coves (*see* Cruising Sydney's Waterways).

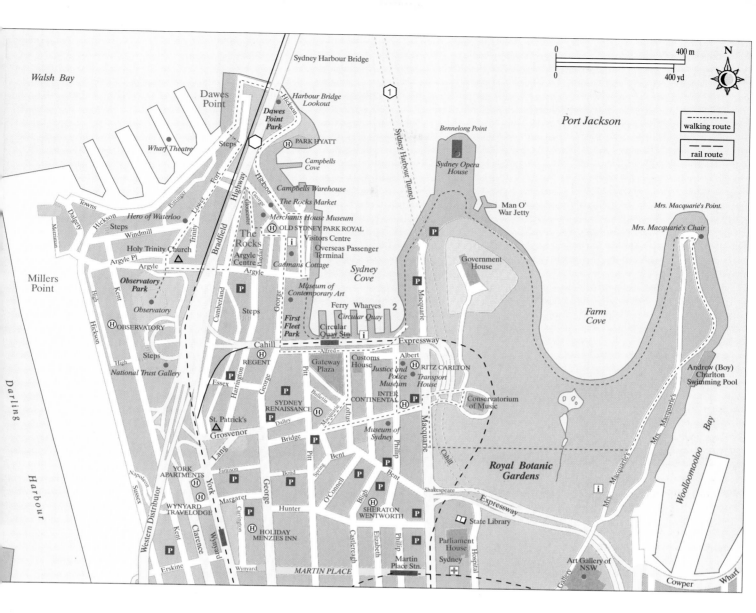

Map of Sydney showing Walsh Bay, Dawes Point, Port Jackson, The Rocks, Sydney Cove, Circular Quay, Royal Botanic Gardens, Farm Cove, Mrs. Macquarie's Point and surrounding streets.

PREVIOUS PAGES *A spectacular panorama of Sydney shows the city's extensive harbour, foreshore suburbs and the high-rise towers.*

OPPOSITE TOP LEFT *George Street is one of the main arteries of the city, running south from Circular Quay into the heart of Sydney.*

OPPOSITE TOP RIGHT *Cadman's Cottage is Sydney's oldest building.*

OPPOSITE CENTRE RIGHT *The Overseas Passenger Terminal at West Circular Quay welcomes passenger liners like the* QE II.

OPPOSITE BOTTOM *A busking Scots piper represents just one of the more than 60 nationalities that make up Sydney's cosmopolitan population.*

RIGHT *The replica of the HMAS* Bounty *docks at Campbells Cove while it awaits passengers for its next cruise around the harbour.*

Birthplace of Sydney

ABOVE *Nestled on the western side of Sydney Cove is the luxurious and architecturally distinctive Park Hyatt Hotel.*

OPPOSITE *The blues of the sky and the harbour's waters help t create the special light that embraces the city.*

Sydney Harbour Bridge – an engineering wonder

Wander around the western boardwalk to where the exclusive **Park Hyatt Sydney Hotel**, with its superlative views of the Opera House across the cove, wraps around the foreshore to Dawes Point, with the **Sydney Harbour Bridge** looming overhead. As you cross into **Dawes Point Park** you see why the bridge has been called the 'engineering wonder of the age'. It was built during the Great Depression of the 1930s and its 504-metre-long steel span arches to a height of 134 metres and weighs 65 000 tonnes. The bridge was constructed from both shores and met over the centre of the harbour with precise accuracy in the winter of 1930. The great granite pylons of the bridge are constructed from rocks quarried 300 kilometres south of the city.

Lower Fort Street – a 19th-century street museum

Continue under the carriageway of the Bradfield Highway to the archaeological dig in the park opposite Lower Fort Street. In 1995 the remains of Sydney's earliest fort, the street's namesake, were discovered in the park. The fo was demolished when the Bridge was being constructed.

The walk up Lower Fort Street reveals one of the city best surviving, 19th-century residential streetscapes. Her Georgian townhouses nestle amongst Victorian terrac homes. On the corner of Windmill Street take a refreshme pause at the **Hero of Waterloo**, an authentic pub built in 184 Legend has it that inebriated patrons were shanghaied b means of a trap door and sent to work as sailors on the hig seas. Mariners were in demand as many ships lay idle in po when the crews absconded to the goldfields.

Continue to **Argyle Place**, the city's only surviving villag green, still surrounded by 19th-century housing. Built b Governor Macquarie in 1810, this tiny park is fronted by th **Holy Trinity Church** (1840), more often called the Garriso Church after the red-coated militia who marched here f prayers every Sunday. Inside are elegant sandstone arch and splendid stained-glass windows.

OPPOSITE FAR LEFT *Silhouetted against the morning sky, the Sydney Opera House rises from the water like the crest of an Australian cockatoo.*

LEFT *Climb to the top of the granite pylons that support the Harbour Bridge for an extensive view of the city and its harbour.*

OPPOSITE CENTRE RIGHT *The Sydney Observatory is ideally placed with magnificent views of the harbour, and its telescopes allow even greater visions into distant universes.*

OPPOSITE BOTTOM RIGHT *The historic Argyle Cut allows passage through the bedrock that supports the Harbour Bridge.*

BELOW *Fire jugglers are just one of many street entertainers who line the foreshore of Sydney Cove, from the Rocks to Circular Quay.*

Sydney Observatory – observations from the top

From Argyle Street take the stairs up to Watson Road and climb up Windmill Hill to Observatory Park for a superb vista of Sydney Harbour stretching away to the west. The copper-domed **Sydney Observatory**, built in 1858, commands a prime spot and features a tower with a time-ball which drops every day at exactly 1pm. The observatory is open for tours, including viewing the night sky via telescopes. There are also exhibits and displays on the science of astronomy.

The drive atop the hill is lined with century-old native fig trees and leads to the **National Trust Centre** (1815), formerly a military hospital, then a high school, and now home to offices, a bookshop and tearooms, and the **S.H. Ervin Gallery**. The gallery features Australian art and culture.

The heart of The Rocks

Return to Argyle Place and walk east on Argyle Street through the **Argyle Cut**. This tunnel was chiselled out of the city's bedrock by convict gangs. At Cumberland Street there are stairs on the right which lead to a pedestrian walkway. The walkway heads across the Sydney Harbour Bridge to the entrance to the **Pylon Lookout**, which is located 200 steps higher in the south-east pylon. This lofty viewpoint affords fabulous sweeping harbour and city views, and houses an historical exhibition on the bridge's construction.

From Cumberland Street head down Gloucester Street to **Susannah Place**, where four terrace houses (numbers 58–64) including a corner store have been recreated by the Historic House Trust to show working-class living conditions at the turn of the century. Susannah Place is open on weekends.

Down the adjacent Cumberland Place stairs is historic **Harrington Street**. The shops at **Clocktower Square** (*see* Shopping) on the western corner of Argyle Street are a great place to shop and browse, as well as those in **The Rocks Square** at the end of Playfair Street; or wander down **Suez Canal**, nicknamed after the old sewer-filled stream which once flowed through here before many of the old hovels were replaced after a plague outbreak in 1900.

Head south on George Street and across First Fleet Park to return to Circular Quay. As you follow the promenade around the cove, past the ferry wharves towards the Sydney Opera House, you'll come upon 50 bronze plaques set into the pavement. This is the **Writers Walk** and it commemorates Sydney and Australia with well-known quotes by Australian and international writers like Patrick White, D.H. Lawrence and Joseph Conrad.

Birthplace of Sydney

Sydney Opera House – a home to sing about

Rightly described as the most significant building of the 20th century, the **Sydney Opera House**, with its gleaming, white sail-like roof, dominates not only Bennelong Point but the psyche of the city itself. Designed by a Danish architect, Jørn Utzon, the building was dogged by controversy, not the least due to its cost which blew out to 13 times the original quote. After its internationally-acclaimed opening in 1973, the problems were forgotten and Sydneysiders basked in the adulation.

Covered with over a million specially engineered tiles, the roof soars as high as a 22-storey building and shelters several concert halls where Australia's premier opera, orchestral and drama companies perform regularly. Tours of the building are conducted daily, jazz bands perform on Sundays on the forecourt, and the exclusive Bennelong Restaurant (*see* Cuisine) is perfect for lunch or dinner with its award-winning, contemporary Australian cuisine and superlative location.

Mrs Macquarie's Chair – a seat for a lady

After lunch follow the foreshore walk around the waterfront of Farm Cove, east of the Opera House, to **Mrs Macquarie's Point**. This point at the eastern extremity of the Domain has wonderful harbour vistas and was, not surprisingly, a favourite spot of the 19th-century governor's wife Elizabeth. Her sandstone seat was carved out of the rock face and still survives.

Royal Botanic Gardens – a green oasis

Enter the **Royal Botanic Gardens**, covering over 30 hectares, through one of its many gates. This city centre oasis showcases a huge collection of native and exotic flora in a stunning setting. Follow the signs to the **Visitor Centre** and the **Gardens Shop**, where guided tours begin and where you can pick up a map and a season guide showing what's flowering, and a list of current events, like the outdoor Shakespeare plays presented on summer evenings (*see* Nightlife).

OPPOSITE *The lush Royal Botanic Gardens is a wonderful place to escape from the hustle and bustle of the city centre.*

TOP *Sydney's most celebrated icons, the Opera House and the Harbour Bridge, are illuminated at daybreak.*

ABOVE *Mrs Macquarie's Chair is where the 19th-century Governor's wife, Elizabeth, would sit and watch the tall-ships sail.*

Established in 1816, the gardens are Australia's oldest scientific institution, and one of the world's leading botanic gardens. Picnickers are fond of the lawns; the paths past the 19th-century statuary are perfect for strolls; and flower lovers enjoy the azalea walk, the rose, herb, native plants and cactus gardens as well as a fernery, and palm groves. Remnants of the continent's first cultivated land survive at the **First Farm Exhibition** and another attraction is the **Sydney Tropical Centre** where a rainforest ecosystem thrives in pyramid and arc glasshouses. You can then reward yourself with tea at the **Botanic Gardens Restaurant** (*see* Cuisine) overlooking the duck pond.

Knightly influences

Exit the gardens at the wrought-iron **Palace Garden Gate** on Macquarie Street which is all that remains of the Garden Palace built for an international exposition in 1879, and which burnt down only three years later. Walk towards the harbour and turn right to the **Conservatorium of Music**, housed in a castle-like building designed by the ex-convict architect, Francis Greenway. The influence, apparently, is after the fashion of a Scottish castle, which would have pleased Scots-born Governor Macquarie who granted Greenway his pardon. Built in 1821 it was originally the governor's grandiose stables until 1913 when the then republic-minded state government returned it to the people.

Located at the end of the adjacent driveway is **Government House** (1838), castellated and turreted, like a throwback to medieval days. This building was also taken from the State Governor in the same year as the Conservatorium of Music. It was later reverted by a subsequent government to vice-regal use, but has recently been returned back to the people and is now open to the public with free admission.

LEFT TOP *The pyramid glasshouse Tropical Centre in the Royal Botanic Gardens allows visitors to enter the world of rainforests and learn more about the continent's ecosystem.*

LEFT CENTRE *Government House has been an important site in the history of the city since the 1840s.*

LEFT *In the heart of the city's stockbroker belt is Macquarie Place Park, where the Obelisk of Distances and the anchor and cannon from the First Fleet's HMS* Sirius *can be found.*

OPPOSITE *Customs House is a handsome sandstone-faced colonial building, the clock face of which is decorated with a trident and dolphin design.*

Prominent buildings and museums

Return to the gates of the Conservatorium, cross Macquarie Street to Bridge Street and you'll find the old **Treasury Building** on the right. Built in the Classical Revival style in 1849, it now forms part of the **Hotel Inter-Continental** and diners can enjoy contemporary cuisine in what was once the historic treasury room (*see* Cuisine).

Walk one block down Bridge Street to the **Museum of Sydney** on the corner of Phillip Street. This is Sydney's latest museum and is built on the ruins of Governor Phillip's original 18th-century Government House, which was exposed by archaeologists in the 1980s and can be seen through a perspex floor. The city's story, from its original Aboriginal inhabitants through the convict days to the present, is depicted through objects, pictures and the latest digital-media technologies.

If you are doing this tour on a Sunday, take a detour down Phillip Street to Albert Street where the **Justice and Police Museum** is located. This 19th-century police station explores the relationship of criminals and law enforcement. Here you can view a bushranger's death mask, inspect forensic evidence from famous crimes and participate in mock trials.

Down Bridge Street is Macquarie Place Park, an historic triangular island surrounded by high-rise office towers. The sandstone **Obelisk of Distances**, dated 1818, marks the point from where all roads were measured in the colonial days. Nearby is the anchor and cannon from HMS *Sirius* which escorted the First Fleet to Sydney back in 1788.

Return to Circular Quay by walking down Loftus Street and past **Customs House**. This historically and architecturally significant building underwent major refurbishment to become a centre for unique cultural activities and culinary experiences. The **Djamu Gallery** showcases the vast Aboriginal, Torres Strait Islander and Pacific collection of the Australian Museum, while the **City Exhibition Space** showcases Sydney's most important buildings and spaces in a high-tech interactive exhibition that includes multimedia displays and an Olympic City exhibiton. Customs House also houses various cafes and restaurants, among them, Cafe Sydney, Section 51 Restaurant and Quay Bar (*see* Cuisine).

Birthplace of Sydney

Heart
of the City

Day Two

Heart of the City

Circular Quay • Sydney Town Hall • Queen Victoria Building • State Theatre • Pitt Street Mall
Sydney Tower • Martin Place • Hyde Park • St Mary's Cathedral • Macquarie Street
Art Gallery of New South Wales • Kings Cross

In this second tour, an exploration of the city centre, you'll find modern skyscrapers and grand Victorian and Georgian colonial buildings, you can wander through Hyde Park, browse through galleries, museums and libraries, pause for refreshments at cafes, and end the day in Kings Cross, Australia's nightlife hub. Beginning at **Circular Quay**, take the CityRail underground to **Town Hall Station**. Trains run every five minutes.

Victorian masterpieces

The **Sydney Town Hall** is an ornate Victorian-baroque edifice completed in 1881, which surprisingly never changed its named to City Hall despite the city's growth. Eleven different architects are said to have contributed to its design, which one critic likened to a 'wedding cake in stone' and a 1960s historian, caught up in that decade's modernist mood, described it as a 'Victorian grotesquerie'. Times change, however, and the Town Hall with its columns, arches, carvings and a 55-metre-high clock tower is one of Sydney's most important landmarks. Inside are stained-glass windows, marble floors and an organ with 8500 pipes, reputed to be one of the world's most powerful.

PREVIOUS PAGES *Hyde Park is a peaceful island in a sea of shops, offices and noisy roadways.*

INSET *The Archibald Fountain in Hyde Park is a popular place for people to meet.*

ABOVE *The bells of St Mary's Cathedral ring out across the city when it hosts weddings and holy celebrations.*

OPPOSITE *The Sydney Town Hall stands symbolically at the crossroads of the city's major thoroughfares.*

Sydney Tower

MLC Centre at Martin P

Hyde Park

St Mary's Cathedral

Macquarie Street

Domain

Mitchell Wing of the State Library

Art Gallery of New South Wales

Cahill Expressway

Tropical Centre

Visitors Centre

Herbarium buildings

Royal Botanic Gardens

Mrs Macquaries Road

Anzac Bridge

Cahill Expressway

Conservatorium of Music

Circular Quay

Government House

Farm Cove

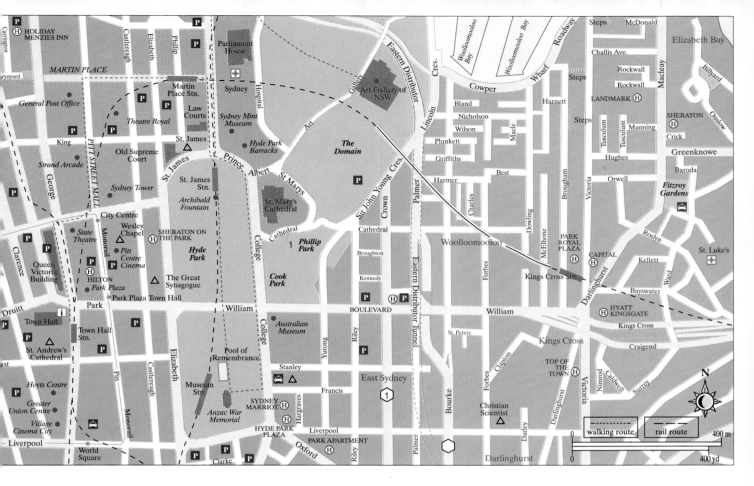

Facing George Street, next to the Town Hall, is
[S]t Andrew's Cathedral, Australia's oldest. The original
[f]oundation stone for this Gothic Revival house of worship was
[la]id by Governor Macquarie in 1819, but it was not until
[a]lmost five decades later that the cathedral was consecrated.
[T]he western towers, designed by the leading colonial architect
[E]dmund Blacket, are best seen from the back of the cathedral,
[w]hich was originally built to face west, not east.

[Q]VB – 'the most beautiful shopping arcade…'

[W]alk back along George Street to view the most spectacular
[b]uilding of Sydney's Victorian era, the **Queen Victoria
[B]uilding**, more commonly referred to as the QVB. Near the
[e]ntrance on the Druitt Street side is a bronze statue of Queen
[V]ictoria. Originally the QVB housed markets, shops, show-
[r]ooms, a concert hall and a coffee palace, but when the

Victorian style was considered outdated, the building was
boarded up for decades. It was revamped with a multi-million-
dollar facelift in the 1980s.

Today this tiered arcade, which covers an entire city block,
is lit again by its glass skylight and topped by 21 copper domes.
The **Royal Clock**, a one-tonne timepiece in the shape of
Balmoral Castle, announces the hour with a quartet of
trumpet-blowing heralds. Pierre Cardin called the
QVB 'themost beautiful shopping arcade in the
world', and few would disagree. Boutique
designer labels and Australian designs offer
abundant shopping choices (*see* Shopping),
and the basement arcade runs underground
all the way from Town Hall station to the
food court of Sydney Plaza, opening out
onto Pitt Street Mall.

---

*REVIEWS PAGES Sydney's CBD, bound by the Botanic Gardens and
Darling Harbour, stretches from Circular Quay to the Town Hall.*

*OPPOSITE   Sydney's stunning Queen Victoria Building provides an
elegant and unique shopping experience.*

RIGHT *This bronze statue of Queen Victoria
stands with sceptre and orb at the entrance to
the famous building named after her, the
QVB, which was built to resemble a
Byzantine palace.*

Heart of the City

OPPOSITE *Thrusting 300 metres into the sky above the city, the Sydney Tower provides the perfect perch to see the city's panorama.*

TOP *Office workers and shoppers are entertained by buskers in the Pitt Street Mall.*

CENTRE *The David Jones store is built in the Art Deco style.*

ABOVE *Martin Place was once a street open to the traffic but it is now a safe corridor for pedestrians.*

State Theatre – a grand picture palace

Emerging at the Market Street end of the QVB, turn right. In the next block you'll find the grand **State Theatre**, built in the movie-mad 1920s when it was hailed as the greatest theatre in the British Empire. This picture palace is unbelievably ornate with an elaborate gilt-vaulted ceiling, marble columns topped by statues of medieval heroes, the world's second-biggest crystal chandelier, and a large and still functioning Wurlitzer organ. The theatre is best appreciated while taking in a movie or a stage show (*see* Nightlife) and guided tours can be arranged.

Pitt Street Mall – a shopping bonanza

Cross Market Street and turn left into the **Pitt Street Mall**, the hub of the city's most popular shopping area (*see* Shopping). Inside **Centrepoint Arcade** on the right is an elevator which will take you to the top of **Sydney Tower** (officially called the AMP Tower), where an observation deck and restaurant are perched atop the metal column which rises over 300 metres (1000 feet) above sea level. The tower offers spectacular 360-degree views of Greater Sydney from the Pacific Ocean to the Blue Mountains. The arcade also connects through to Castle-reagh Street where **David Jones** (*see* Shopping), Sydney's most famous department store, can be found. David Jones is renowned for its old-style service, elaborate Christmas decorations and its original 1920s building with marble floors and stylish fittings. It is Sydney's answer to London's Harrods.

On the left side of Pitt Street Mall are **Grace Bros** and **Sydney Plaza**, which has a large food court that connects with the QVB, and a little further down, the **Strand Arcade** (*see* Shopping), a 19th-century shopping arcade which was reconstructed after being gutted by fire in the 1970s. A good place to stop for a 'cuppa' is **Harris Coffee and Tea** (*see* Cuisine), an old-fashioned cafe with smoked-glass windows and copper samovars.

Martin Place – a pedestrian thoroughfare

Cross King Street, the hub of internationally renowned designer boutiques (*see* Shopping), and walk one block to **Martin Place**, a wide pedestrian thoroughfare with an amphitheatre, fountains, sculptures, and barrow flower and newspaper sellers. Martin Place stretches from George Street to Macquarie Street and is flanked by the sleek high-rise towers of the nation's premier banking institutions. Bordered by Pitt and George streets is the **General Post Office**, crowned by a fine clock and bell tower. The GPO was built between 1866 and 1874 and was renovated in 1999, now featuring a shopping arcade on the ground floor.

Walk east up Martin Place to historic **Macquarie Street**. Turn right and walk south to **Queens Square**, where statues of Queen Victoria and her consort Prince Albert stand on either side. In the 1890s republicans held public meetings here and railed against the monarchy – a century later the debate still rages. On the right is **St James' Church**, built in 1820 by Francis Greenway, an architect who was transported from England for forgery. Sydney's oldest-surviving ecclesiastical building features a square tower and copper spire. Marble memorials around the interior walls commemorate eminent colonial parishioners, including the commander of the ship *Dunbar*, who perished along with all the passengers and crew, save one, when a 'fearful gale' wrecked the boat on Sydney Heads in 1857. Next door to St James' is the **Old Supreme Court** building, Australia's second-oldest courthouse, also built by Greenway in the same year.

Hyde Park – a leafy retreat

Across St James Road is **Hyde Park**, named after its London counterpart. Originally much larger, the park was fenced during Governor Macquarie's term of office in 1810 when it was the site of the colony's first horseraces. At lunchtime city workers converge on the lawns of Hyde Park, shaded by huge fig trees with buttressed roots, for impromptu picnics, a quiet nap, a game of chess at the outdoor venue, or take time out to work on a suntan. All paths within the park lead to the **Archibald Fountain**, located at the northern end where a bronze Apollo overlooks other mythological figures which represent the nation's past and future. The story of the fountain, designed by the French sculptor Francois Sicard in 1933, is explained on a plaque. The 'Archibald' was donated by the philanthropic publisher of the same name and is a favourite meeting place. If you follow the tree-lined Avenue of Remembrance across Park Street you'll come to the **Anzac War Memorial** at the southern end of Hyde Park. This 30-metre-high, Art Deco-style memorial is dedicated to the Australian and New Zealand Army Corps (ANZAC) who fought together during World War 1.

LEFT TOP *With over 8 million exhibits, children of all ages enjoy visiting the Australian Museum of Natural History, one of the world's finest.*

LEFT *The Anzac War Memorial in Hyde Park stands as a monument to the bravery and loyalty of troops during World War I.*

OPPOSITE TOP *The wall surrounding the Archibald Fountain provides great seat to catch up on the news.*

OPPOSITE BOTTOM *Designed by Francis Greenway, the Hyde Park Barracks have been restored so that visitors can appreciate the convict experience.*

Lofty buildings

From Hyde Park cross College Street to the famous **Australian Museum** housed inside an impressive 1849 building. This natural history museum is rated as one of the best in the world with a wide range of exhibitions including displays of the country's fauna and flora, dinosaurs, Aboriginal Australia, fossils, and a hands-on section popular with children.

Walk north along College Street, cross William Street, and you'll come to St Mary's Cathedral, the world's sixth-largest. Work on this Gothic Revival cathedral began in 1868 and continued, over the next 130-odd years. Work on the final stage, the addition of the spires to the southern end, began in 1999. The steel frames, each 27 metres high, were lifted onto the towers by helicopter. Notable features within this spiritual domain include flying buttresses, a huge High Altar, and the mosaic in the Sanctuary.

Hyde Park Barracks – quarters fit for convicts

Cross St Marys Road north of the cathedral and walk back to the corner of Macquarie Street. The entrance to **Hyde Park Barracks** is on the right. This handsome brick building is the best example of the pardoned, convict-architect Greenway. It is a classic Georgian style with a three-storey barracks built in 1817 during the term of the energetic and visionary Governor Macquarie, whose name appears above the clock in the front gable. Convicts previously put up in lodgings at The Rocks were moved to the Barracks in order to control their time and labour more efficiently. Over the decades, when it became a female immigrants' shelter and later government offices, other buildings were erected in the walled compound, but these were demolished when the Hyde Park Barracks was restored during 1980–84. The building now stands unadorned and looks like its original splendid self.

An outdoor cafe (*see* Cuisine) at the barracks is a pleasant spot for morning tea or lunch, after or before exploring the museum. Hammocks strung up in the top floor show where the 600 convicts slept, and fascinating displays chronicle how the barracks' occupants went about their daily lives. Ask about **Convict Experience Tours** where participants sleep over in the hammocks, and also the **Tried and Transported Tour**, which combines a mock trial at the **Justice and Police Museum**, a two-hour 'transportation' sail on the tall-ship *Solway Lass*, as well as the sleep over.

Macquarie Street – an historic street

Macquarie Street is one of Sydney's most significant historical streets. Next door to the barracks is an attractive colonial building, fronted by a colonnaded timber verandah, which houses the **Sydney Mint Museum**. The original coining machines used when the Royal Mint was operating from 1853 to 1927 are on display at the museum and visitors can mint their own sovereigns, see exhibitions on the lure of gold, rare coins, and priceless objects made of gold and silver.

Prior to the gold rush of the 1850s the Mint served as part of the Rum Hospital, Sydney's first hospital built in 1812. The present **Sydney Hospital**, next door, replaced the early building in 1879 and the design of its nurses' quarters is believed to have been sanctioned by Florence Nightingale. Visitors can rub the nose of **Il Porcellino**, the brass boar outside fashioned after the famous original in Florence, and toss a coin into the water at the boar's base for good luck.

the first to popularise the name Australi
instead of New Holland, its previous titl
Beside the statue is a plaque and a poem penne
by Flinders in honour of his cat Trim, wh
accompanied him on all his journeys.

The imposing stone building behind thi
statue is the **State Library of New South Wale**
which can be entered by the new glass additio
on Macquarie Street. The best entrance
though, is around the corner where
magnificent portico, designed in the classica
Greek style, marks the entrance to the **Mitche**
wing. The bronze doors are embossed wit
famous explorers and Aboriginal cultura
scenes and the foyer has a superb mosaic floo
which recreates an intriguing early map of th
Australian continent by the Dutch explorer, Abel Tasman
Lit by a skylight, the 50-metre-long reading room i
encircled by tiers of books, part of the initial bequest c
61 000 books, which include rare manuscripts like Captai
Cook's journals, donated to the library in 1906 by it
benefactor, lawyer David Scott Mitchell. An undergroun
tunnel connects the Mitchell to the newer library wing,
cafe, exhibition areas, and an excellent bookshop.

Heading north on Macquarie Street is the **State Parliament House**, also once part of the Rum Hospital, reputed to be the world's oldest continuously-used parliamentary building. The first session sat here in 1829. Visitors can sit in the public galleries when parliament is in session.

Continue north along Macquarie Street and you will find a bronze statue of the sea-explorer **Matthew Flinders**, the first man to circumnavigate the continent during 1801–3, and

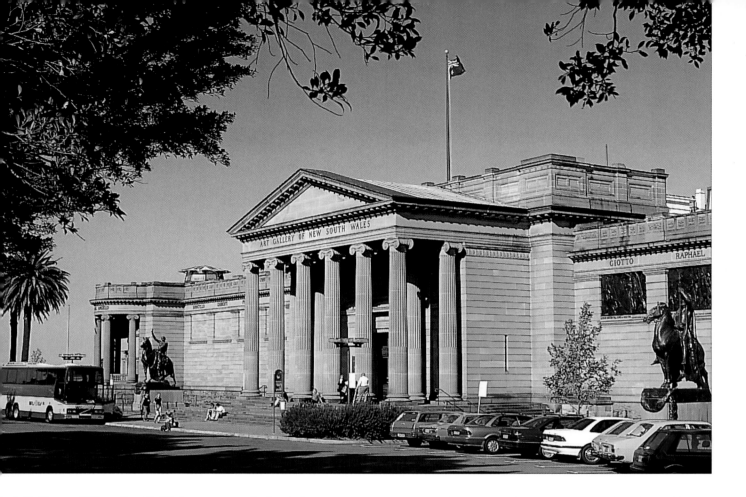

Art Gallery of New South Wales – an artistic vision

From the Mitchell walk east and cross Hospital Road to The Domain. This grassy space overlooks the Royal Botanic Gardens across the Cahill Expressway, the main traffic artery from the Harbour Bridge to the eastern suburbs. Walk directly across The Domain to the Art Gallery of New South Wales with its grand Ionic colonnades. Designed by W.L. Vernon, the Government architect in 1909, the gallery houses the world's largest permanent exhibition of Aboriginal art, and paintings by well-known Australian and international artists.

The Gallery Shop (*see* Shopping) has Australia's best range of art books as well as posters, cards and gifts. The Gallery Cafe (*see* Cuisine), is a splendid place for coffee or lunch. It overlooks Woolloomooloo Bay and its long finger wharf which, until its redevelopment in 1997, remained the world's largest surviving historic finger wharf. Opposite the wharf, on Cowper Wharf Road, is Harry's Cafe de Wheels, an all night pie wagon that has been frequented by generations of hungry revellers. The original wagon now resides in the Powerhouse Museum in Ultimo. From Harry's, Cowper Wharf Road extends around the bay to the naval facilities at Garden Island, the high-rise apartments of Potts Point, and along the ridge to Kings Cross (*see* Nightlife), an ideal destination for a great night out on the town.

OPPOSITE TOP *Parliament House, built by Macquarie in 1816, stands at the top section of Macquarie Street. The state of New South Wales has been run from this Georgian building since 1829.*

OPPOSITE BOTTOM *The old wing of the State Library of New South Wales, otherwise known as the Mitchell Library, faces the Botanic Gardens and contains the largest collection of Australiana in the world. It was created from David Mitchell's extensive 19th-century collection.*

ABOVE *The Art Gallery of New South Wales houses a wonderful collection ranging from early watercolours of the colony, a substantial Aboriginal collection, and works by Australia's best contemporary artists to famous European masters including Picasso and Rembrandt.*

Heart of the City

ABOVE *Kings Cross turned from a leafy suburb to a nightlife centre in the 1960s with the arrival of US troops on leave from Vietnam. Today, it is a bustling district which turns on the glitz at night with services advertised by colourful neons.*

LEFT *While the Cross has always been a centre for rebels, radicals, revolutionaries, crooks, cranks and crims – in fact a chocolate-box assortment of humanity – it is still a major tourist attraction with many excellent hotels, backpacker accommodation, chic cafes and fine restaurants.*

OPPOSITE *Shining like a beacon, the big red-and-white Coke sign at the top of William Street marks the entrance to the Cross and invites tourists to experience the vibrant mixture of bars and nightclubs where they can party until dawn.*

Kings Cross – a lively centre

The 'Cross' is easy to get to. Just hop on a **Sydney Explorer Bus**, which stops outside the Art Gallery, and get off in **Darlinghurst Road**, the neon hub of Australia's most notorious area, where adults-only clubs and late-night restaurants cater for the crowds 24 hours a day. Alternatively, you can walk back to Martin Place and catch the underground to Kings Cross station. Away from the 'sleaze strip' Kings Cross has leafy back lanes, especially along Victoria Street, where elegant terrace houses are adjoined to 1930s apartments and guest houses, which now cater for backpackers.

If you have time to spare, reboard the Sydney Explorer in **Macleay Street** and get off at **Elizabeth Bay House** on Onslow Avenue. Once 'the finest house in the colony', this elegant Regency mansion, built in 1832, is furnished in the Georgian style and overlooks Elizabeth Bay, surrounded by exclusive apartments and walled residences. This historic home hosts a number of exhibitions and most of its rooms are open for inspection by the public. Walk up to Kings Cross for a night out, or return to Circular Quay via the Sydney Explorer or the 311 bus.

Heart of the City

Darling Harbour
and Chinatown

Day Three

DARLING HARBOUR AND CHINATOWN

Sydney Aquarium • Cockle Bay • National Maritime Museum
Harbourside Marketplace • Sydney Fish Markets • Powerhouse Museum
Chinatown • Chinese Garden • Glebe • Sydney University • Star City Casino

The focus for the third day is the inner south-west of the city where many of Sydney's newest and most popular tourist attractions are found in suburbs that were formerly neglected. **Darling Harbour**, a vibrant urban redevelopment loosely modelled on Boston and Baltimore's waterfront makeovers, is renowned for its contemporary architecture, museums, aquarium, shops, restaurants, and entertainment program.

Sydney Aquarium – a shark attraction
Near the ferry wharf on the eastern side of Darling Harbour is **Sydney Aquarium**. The architect Phillip Cox, responsible for much of Darling Harbour's bold designs, came up with the novel idea of submerging the fish tanks into the harbour. This not only reduces costs by keeping the water pressure of the tanks balanced, it also provides visitors with the unique experience of an underwater descent. At the Open Ocean exhibit onlookers are able to walk through the underwater tunnels and become surrounded by one of the world's largest shark collections. Other exhibits include a sanctuary for marine mammals, a coral reef with tropical fish and a mangrove wetland complete with crocodiles.

PREVIOUS PAGES *The Harbour Festival Marketplace is an ultra-modern structure housing shops and restaurants.*

INSET *The pagoda gate marks the entrance to Chinatown, with its array of restaurants, traditional medicine and grocery stores.*

ABOVE *As the sun sets over the city, lights bring to life the foreshor promenade of Darling Harbour, built around Cockle Bay.*

OPPOSITE *A magnificent glass archway provides a unique entranc to the Harbour Festival Marketplace, across the water from the cit*

Sydney Tower

Western Distributor

Passenger Shipping Terminal

Sydney Aquarium

Darling Harbour

National Maritime Museum

Pyrmont

Sydney Casino

Novotel Hotel

Cockle Bay

Pyrmont Bridge

Chinatown

Ultimo

Cockle Bay Wharf – restaurants and nightlife

This complex on the city side of Darling Harbour adds another dimension to an area which is otherwise focused mainly on tourist and family entertainment. Including top-notch restaurants aimed at the high end of town, such as Ampersand, and the hip, Malaysian-style Chinta Ria Temple of Love (*see* Cuisine), the complex also houses the world-famous nightclub, Home (*see* Nightlife).

To get to the western side of Darling Harbour walk across Cockle Bay, where convicts used to look for molluscs, via the old **Pyrmont Bridge**. The bridge was closed to vehicular traffic in 1981 and has an electrically powered steel span, described as a wonder of its age in 1902, which once opened to allow access for large ships into the harbour. Alternatively take the **monorail**, which leaves every few minutes on a circular track that includes a run across the Pyrmont Bridge.

National Maritime Museum – Australia's oceanic past

Beside the Harbourside Monorail station at the end of Pyrmont Bridge is the **National Maritime Museum**. The museum is a tribute to Australia's maritime past and present, and combines floating and indoor exhibits from Aboriginal fishing techniques to the evolution of the modern surfboard and the history of the bikini. You can experience life on a convict ship or explore below decks on an Australian Navy destroyer, the largest of the maritime exhibits. Other exhibits include a pearling lugger, a Vietnamese refugee ship and the world's fastest boat built by a Sydneysider in his backyard.

PREVIOUS PAGES *Darling Harbour i a spectacular example of Sydney extensive urban redevelopment.*

ABOVE *Don't forget to take a 21s century ride on the monorail from th centre of the city, across Pyrmont Bridg to Darling Harbour.*

OPPOSITE TOP *A myriad sparkling ligh light up the buildings surrounding Cock Bay, showing another side to Sydney multifaceted personality.*

OPPOSITE BOTTOM *Yachts moor outsid the National Maritime Museum, whic examines Australia's relationship wit the sea from the early days to the presen*

A feast of eateries and shops

A stroll around Cockle Bay Promenade will bring you to the **Harbourside Festival Marketplace**. Within its unique arched glass entry are an abundance of souvenir shops (*see* Shopping) and a range of eateries from Japanese sushi bars to American spare ribs (*see* Cuisine). At the front of the building are several excellent restaurants and bars which face the promenade and harbour, adding to the relaxed holiday atmosphere.

Next, walk or take the monorail to Convention Station and then stroll across Pyrmont Street to the Harris Street Car Park, which houses the **Harris Street Motor Museum**. The museum is a must for car lovers. Displaying over 175 different vehicles, dating from 1899 to the present, it tells the story of the Australian car industry.

For an exciting detour, as well as the best seafood lunch in Sydney, walk north along Harris Street, turn left into Gipps Street and under the overhead expressway to the **Sydney Fish Markets**. The markets overlook Blackwattle Bay, which is traversed by the stunning new **Anzac Bridge**. An incredible array of seafood is on display from Balmain Bugs – unique to Sydney Harbour – to barramundi airlifted from Darwin. You can buy take-away fish and chips from Doyles (*see* Cuisine), Japanese sashimi, seafood kebabs, or grilled octopus from a variety of outlets, and eat at the tables overlooking the sparkling waters of the bay. Upstairs from the markets is the Sydney Seafood School which runs one-day workshops in seafood cooking, from Thai to Cajun, and operates tours of the markets.

Powerhouse Museum – a core of technology

Those feeling energetic can return to Harris Street and walk south four blocks to get to the **Powerhouse Museum**. Alternatively, return to Darling Harbour, catch the monorail to Haymarket Station, then walk across the pedestrian ramp to one of the world's great museums and Australia's largest.

The Powerhouse focuses on technology, social history, decorative arts and science, and also encourages visitor participation in interactive exhibits including a chance to star in a spectacular movie sequence that participants can take home on a video cassette. The museum takes its name from the old powerhouse buildings which compose its core including the Victorian-era boiler house and turbine hall – original brick structures over 80 metres long and 28 metres wide. Exhibits include life in colonial bush huts, working locomotives, a walk-in computer and a World War II Catalina flying boat with a 32-metre wing span, which is the largest suspended object in any museum worldwide.

OPPOSITE TOP *The Sydney Fish Markets are a seafood lover's gastronomic paradise, with cafes and restaurants serving the freshest produce the sea has to offer.*

OPPOSITE CENTRE *Trawlers return to the Sydney Fish Markets daily to unload catches which have been brought in from the Pacific Ocean depths.*

OPPOSITE BOTTOM *The Powerhouse Museum is a fascinating technological theme park. It is both an educational and entertaining experience.*

Darling Harbour and Chinatown

ABOVE   *The Dong Seng Souvenir shop in Chinatown is just one of the many unusual retai*
establishments that bring the culture and flavour of the East to the centre of a western metropolis.

LEFT   *Two Chinese lions sit at the base of the pagoda which marks the entrance to Dixon Street.*
a pedestrian mall which is the hub of Sydney's Chinatown.

OPPOSITE TOP   *The Chinese Gardens at Darling Harbour allow the visitors to wander through*
walled haven that is reminiscent of 5th-century Chinese emperors' gardens.

54

Chinatown – an Asian experience

From the museum return to the Haymarket monorail station and walk down Hay Street. This street was one of the original borders of Sydney's **Chinatown** which has now spread out from its centre, **Dixon Street**, to encompass the surrounding area from Liverpool Street in the north to Pitt Street in the east and south to Central Railway Station. This is a fascinating area to explore. Traditional pharmacists write out prescriptions for bones and seeds, supermarkets stock exclusively Asian products, dry-goods merchants deal in exotic foodstuffs like salted fish and shark fins, and jewellers sell 18-carat gold necklaces and jade amulets. Every second shop in Chinatown is a restaurant and people all over Sydney flock here to shop, eat and enjoy the nightlife. It is also a popular place to eat before going to see a show at the nearby **Entertainment Centre** on Harbour Street. Chinatown is at its noisiest and most colourful during Chinese New Year, but is also crowded on Sunday mornings for traditional yum cha lunch described as 'an exotic moveable feast' (*see* Cuisine).

Wander north up Dixon Street, through the pagoda gate that marks the entrance to Chinatown, and across Harbour Street for the **Chinese Garden** set in the south-east corner of the Darling Harbour complex. Designed in a Taoist Cantonese style, which originated in the 5th century, the gardens represent 'eternity' and measure 10 000 square metres. They were given to Australia as a bicentennial gift from the Guangdong province in 1988 and include a rambling watercourse, a three-tiered pagoda, a waterside pavilion, a 'courtyard of repose', a rock forest, and a teahouse serving tea and cakes, both Chinese and Western. At the entrance stands a duo of green-granite guardian lions that symbolise the partnership between Guangzhou (Canton) and Sydney.

A little detour

Chinatown is a favourite place for an evening meal but, if you prefer a more eclectic menu, **Glebe**, a nearby inner-city suburb, offers a variety of cosmopolitan eateries (*see* Cuisine). To get to Glebe, renowned also for its eccentric student population, bookshops, Victorian architecture, and mansions-turned-backpacker lodgings, take the number 431 or the 434 State Transit bus from George Street, along Parramatta Road to Glebe Point Road.

Also worth a detour is **Sydney University**, reached by travelling further along Parramatta Road (bus numbers 438, 440, 468, 470). This is Australia's oldest, and most prestigious tertiary institution; it sprawls over three suburbs, runs for a kilometre along Parramatta Road, and includes sports fields and a variety of buildings. Its best architecture is the old central block enclosing a quadrangle, built in Victorian Gothic style in 1854 and modelled after the Oxbridge-medieval tradition. The clocktower and carillon are admirable, the antiquities in the **Nicholson Museum** are worth exploring, and the vaulted roof of the **Grand Hall** where graduation ceremonies are held is impressive.

Star City Casino – time for a nightcap

To finish up the evening after dinner at either Chinatown or Glebe the obvious venue would be the fabulously situated **Star City Casino** (*see* Nightlife). Just five minutes walk from the National Maritime Museum, the casino offers all the glamour and glitz of an exciting evening out and beautiful serene views overlooking the inner harbour.

OPPOSITE TOP *The spectacular Anzac Bridge is a vision of the 21st century and the latest monument to grace Sydney.*

OPPOSITE BOTTOM *The Convent Garden Hotel in Chinatown took its name from the famous London district; it is a great place to have a quiet ale.*

ABOVE *Glebe Point Road is a stylish inner-city main street that provides an eclectic mix of shops for locals and visitors alike.*

Bondi and the Eastern Suburbs

Day Four

$\mathcal{B}$ONDI AND THE EASTERN SUBURBS

Double Bay • Heritage Foreshore Track • Vaucluse House • Watsons Bay • The Gap
Bondi Beach • Coogee Beach • Randwick Racecourse • Sydney Cricket Ground
Paddington • Centennial Park • Fox Studios • Taylor Square

The fourth day of touring Sydney circles the eclectic east and includes the luxurious harbourside suburb of Double Bay; the southern beaches, including famous Bondi Beach; Paddington, renowned for its Victorian terrace houses, art galleries and cafes; and Darlinghurst, a hub of nightlife activity.

Explorer Bus – sweeping east
The best place to start is by boarding the **Explorer Bus** for its Bondi route at the **Sydney Buses Ticket Kiosk** at Circular Quay. From the Quay it passes the **Royal Botanic Gardens**, curves around **Woolloomooloo Bay**, winds up through **Potts Point** and **Kings Cross**, and heads east on **New South Head Road**, the main artery to the Eastern Suburbs.

At picturesque **Rushcutters Bay** yachts crowd the marinas of the **Cruising Yacht Club**; the scene is a far cry from the early days when convicts came to cut rushes for roof-thatching in the swamps behind the bay where the park now stands. The route veers left around the foreshores to elegant **Darling Point**, Sydney's most expensive real estate area. Here grand old mansions rub shoulders with luxury apartment blocks. On the left look out for **St Mark's Anglican Church**, built in the Victorian Gothic style in 1848 by the eminent architect Edmund Blacket. It is located on the corner of Greenoaks Avenue and Darling Point Road and is auspicious because a number of Sydney's socialites and the occasional superstar, like Elton John, have recited their nuptial vows at its altar.

PREVIOUS PAGES *Surfers take advantage of perfect offshore winds to ride the waves into Sydney's famous Bondi Beach.*

INSET *The Gap at Watsons Bay comprises sandstone cliffs formed by the pounding of the ocean on the continent's eastern perimeter.*

Double Bay – exclusive waterfront suburbs

At **Double Bay** expensive boutiques cater for some of the biggest names in haute couture, and elegant restaurants and sidewalk cafes are the chic places to be seen. An espresso at the **Cosmo Terrace Cafe** (*see* Cuisine), haunt of high society in Knox Street, is a great place to watch the passing parade. The cafe scene, reminiscent of Europe, began here during World War II when European immigrants and refugees moved into the area bringing their cosmopolitan cultures with them and revitalising Sydney's formerly Anglicised society.

Reboard the bus and enjoy the harbour views as the road climbs to **Point Piper**, another exclusive waterfront suburb, and drops down to spacious **Rose Bay**, where the occasional sea plane still lands. Until the 1970s flying boats used to take off for Lord Howe Island from this stretch of water. From the wharf, ferries run back to Circular Quay and to **Watsons Bay** further along the bus route. As the bus climbs up from Rose Bay, the prominent **Sacred Heart Convent** can be seen. This is a Roman Catholic college built by the eccentric architect Horbury Hunt, who died a pauper in 1904 after losing his fortune in the economic depression of the 1890s.

Heritage Foreshore Track – a water's edge stroll

Alight at the convent and walk down Bayview Hill Road and into the lane of the same name for an interesting one-kilometre saunter around the **Heritage Foreshore Track**. The walk affords wonderful vistas of the harbour and also allows for intimate peeks at the grand harbourside residences as it winds around tiny **Hermit Bay** to **Nielsen Park** with its shaded lawns, tearooms, and a sandy cove, which is netted for safe swimming – probably because of its ominous name, **Shark Beach**.

Vaucluse House – in grand style

For those not wishing to take the walk, the Explorer Bus also winds around to Nielsen Park, then on to **Vaucluse Bay**, named after the historic **Vaucluse House**. This grand house was once the residence of William Charles Wentworth, the 'father of the Australian constitution', and is located on nearby Wentworth Road. Overlooking the harbour and surrounded by 11 hectares of beautiful gardens, the castellated, Gothic-style residence was built in 1803 and has been a museum ever since the Wentworth family passed it on to the state government in 1910. The lavishly decorated interior includes floor tiles imported from Pompeii and furnishings from the Doge's Palace in Venice. The lifestyle of the servants who once worked at Vaucluse House is also depicted in the kitchen wing, stables and outbuildings.

OPPOSITE *High-rise apartments overlook Double Bay, a cosmopolitan suburb with some of Sydney's most exclusive addresses.*

ABOVE *The Explorer Bus offers visitors the 'chauffeur-driven' way to experience the Eastern Suburbs.*

BELOW *Charming Rushcutters Bay is a popular mooring area for sailors who enjoy Sydney's waterways.*

Sydney Tower

Royal Botanic

Potts Point

Elizabeth Bay

Rushcutters Bay

Double Bay

Sydney Harbour Bridge

Sydney Opera House

North Sydney

Garden Island

Darling Point

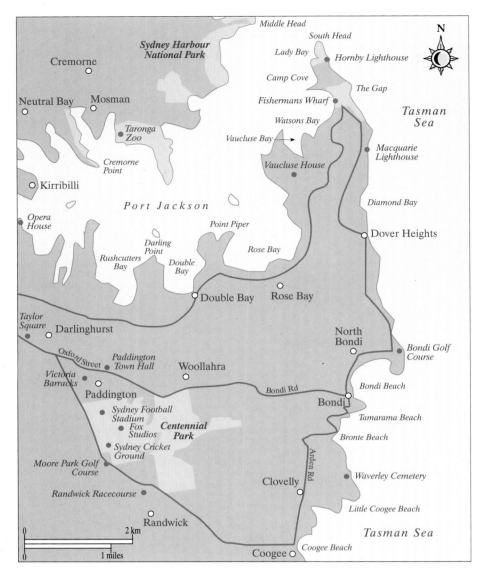

ferries return to Circular Quay via Ros
Bay. On the beachside north of the wharf i
Sydney's best-known seafood restauran
Doyles (*see* Cuisine). The restaurant is sti
run by the descendants of the first fishin
family who began the business in 1885.

Before you reward yourself with lunc
take a bracing walk to or from **South Hea**
with its fabulous clifftop viewpoints o
Sydney Harbour. You can also walk to **Th**
Gap, which has the dubious reputation a
being the city's favourite suicide spot. ⁄
return walk from Watsons Bay is about thre
kilometres and takes about an hour and a half. Alternativel
you could catch the bus to **The Gap Park** or from Watson
Bay walk straight up through **Robertson Park** and acros
Military Road to Sydney's most notorious lookout, and the
walk back to Watsons Bay via South Head.

At The Gap the ocean churns against a rock she
hundreds of metres below a sheer cliff drop and the view
are awe-inspiring. The walkway heads north to South Hea
past **Hornby Lighthouse** on the clifftop; it was built in 185
after two passenger boats were wrecked off the Heads wit
a great loss of life. This lookout is a favourite vantage poi
for watching the **Sydney to Hobart Ocean Yacht Race** hel
every Boxing Day (*see* Events). The trail then winds aroun
the rocks past the secluded **Lady Bay Beach**, one of Sydney
official nude beaches, which overlooks the entrance t
Sydney Harbour, past sandy **Camp Cove**, then throug
native bushland back to Watsons Bay.

Rumour has it that Wentworth, who had a phobia for snakes, dug out a trench around the property and filled it with imported Irish soil, believing that this would deter the feared reptile. Nothing is written about the success or otherwise of this undertaking, but local food critics have written extensively on the quality of the cuisine served in the **Vaucluse House Tearooms**, a perfect spot for morning tea. Travellers interested in historic buildings should purchase a 'Ticket Through Time'. Its cost is minimal and it allows the holder unlimited access to all Historic Houses Trust properties.

South Head – clifftop vantage points

The next stop is **Watsons Bay**, the last settlement on the southern harbour foreshores, located on the western side of the thin promontory of land between the Pacific Ocean and Sydney Harbour. Swimming baths are at the southern end of the bay and in the centre is **Fisherman's Wharf**, where

PREVIOUS PAGES *Jutting out into the harbour, Darling Point is million-dollar real estate. High-rise luxury apartments are surrounded by magnificent homes and gardens, many with enviable harbour views and private moorings.*

ABOVE *The renowned Doyles Seafood Restaurant on the sands of Watsons Bay lends a feel of the French Riviera to the quiet cove.*

TOP *The Hornby Lighthouse perched on South Head marks the entrance to Sydney Harbour. South Head is a great place to visit and watch marine craft of all sizes enter and leave the harbour.*

RIGHT *The Pacific Ocean abuts the coastline of the Eastern Suburbs. Inside the harbour are the white sands of Camp Cove, Watsons Bay and the broad band of Rose Bay.*

Bondi Beach – a famous curve of sand

Reboard the Explorer at Watsons Bay Park and travel south along the Pacific coast past **Macquarie Lighthouse**, Sydney's main navigation beacon and the first lighthouse built on Australian soil. The bus travels past the luxury clifftop suburb of **Dover Heights**, the **Bondi Golf Course** which must, surely, be one of the world's most spectacular locations at which to tee off, and down to Australia's most renowned stretch of sand, **Bondi Beach**.

Bondi is located 8 kilometres from Sydney, the closest ocean beach to the city, and has attracted the crowds for over a century. Trams once ran to the beachfront and in the 1930s and 40s, when cars were still a rarity, Bondi Beach hosted enormous weekend crowds of up to 40 000 beach-goers who packed the sands on hot summer days. Today, motorists can choose from dozens of beaches up and down the coast, but Bondi is still a favourite and is fast becoming a chic residential area for young professionals. The spacious sands are wonderful for sunbathing, lazing with a pulp novel, or for voyeurism, while a dip in the surf is *de rigueur* for the essential Sydney experience.

Since the early century Bondi has been patrolled by volunteer lifesavers, and their summer beach carnivals – when rival clubs compete in rescue operations and surf boat and swimming races – are a thrilling addition to the visitor's calendar of 'must-see' events. Bondi attracts a diverse and cosmopolitan crowd and the beachside promenade is great for people watching and for catching skateboarders and rollerbladers delighting the crowds with their daredevil antics. **Campbell Parade**, which wraps around behind the beach, is lined with hotels, restaurants, bars, and cafes and is a popular venue for Saturday night drinking and dining, and lazy Sunday brunch. For views and people watching and some of Sydney's most renowned contemporary cuisine, opt for lunch on the balcony at **Ravesi's** (*see* Cuisine) on the corner of Campbell Parade and Hall Street. For wonderful panoramas of Bondi and a chance to birdwatch – keep a lookout for albatrosses and other seabirds – take the two-kilometre-return walk around the ocean front from South Bondi to Tamarama Bay.

LEFT *A surfer rides a Pacific wave into the eastern beaches.*

RIGHT *There are over 34 ocean beaches within the boundary of Sydney. This is Bondi Beach, the continent's most famous sweep of sand.*

Bondi and the Eastern Suburbs   66

The Southern Beaches

Continuing on from Bondi, the bus hugs the coast heading south towards **Bronte**, a surfing beach backed by grassy parklands popular with weekend picnickers. It then passes the clifftop **Waverley Cemetery**, where many famous Australians, including the writers Henry Lawson and Henry Kendall, are buried. The narrow bay at **Clovelly** is the next stop and is excellent for swimming and very popular with divers.

Coogee Beach, further on, is less crowded than Bondi and offers expansive sands and salt-water swimming pools including the newly restored **Wylie's Baths**, built in 1907. Coogee was fashionable early this century but then fell out of favour. Now the wheel has turned once again; real estate prices

have soared, cafes line the beachfront road, and former guest-houses have opened their doors to backpackers.

A sporting edge

From Coogee, the Explorer Bus heads back towards the city via the **Royal Randwick Racecourse**. This is Sydney's premier racecourse and is a must for visitors who enjoy the excitement and glamour of the 'sport of kings', especially during Sydney's colourful Autumn and Spring Racing Carnivals (*see* Events). The first race meetings at Randwick commenced in 1860.

The bus route then heads north along the Anzac Parade, passing **Moore Park Golf Course** on the left, to the **Sydney Cricket Ground** and **Sydney Football Stadium**. Sport lovers can watch World Series Cricket during summer, and rugby league and rugby union matches in winter. On non-match days tours of both the Sydney Football Stadium and the Sydney Cricket Ground are on offer, and include the cricket museum where 'talking ghosts' of cricket legends discuss topics, like the infamous Bodyline Test series between England and Australia, continuing with the players dressing rooms and the historic stands.

At the top end of Paddington, just opposite where Moore Park Road meets Oxford Street, is enormous **Centennial Park**, 220 hectares of open space which is very popular with joggers, cyclists, roller-bladers, horse-riders and picnickers. The English-style park was given its name in 1888 to celebrate Australia's centenary.

Just outside Centennial Park, on Lang Road, is **Fox Studios**, a large complex that includes the restaurants, entertainment, markets, live broadcast and retail shops of Bent Street, 12 Hoyts cinemas which feature VIP lounges and stadium seating, and the Fox Studios Backlot which offers fans of the big- and small-screen the chance to go behind the scenes of movie-making.

Opposite the Oxford Street Gates of Centennial Park is **Queen Street**, which runs through **Woollahra**, Paddington's wealthy neighbouring suburb. Queen Street is famous for its antique shops and art galleries (see Shopping). Pick up a copy of the Paddington Galleries Guide and Map from galleries and tourist offices (or phone 9332–1840) for information on the 34 galleries in the Paddington region.

OPPOSITE TOP *Take some time out to feed the ducks at Centennial Park.*

OPPOSITE BOTTOM *Coogee Beach looks fabulous in the first light of the day.*

TOP *Royal Randwick Racecourse is a great place to spend a sunny Saturday trying your luck on the horses or just indulging in the atmosphere and enjoying a glass of champagne.*

ABOVE *The cemetery at Waverley sits upon a headland overlooking the ocean, providing a marvellous resting place for many of Sydney's historical characters, including Henry Lawson and Henry Kendall.*

Bondi and the Eastern Suburbs

ABOVE *Oxford Street is alive with cafes, bars and restaurants and a large number of Sydney's designer boutiques.*

BELOW *Paddington Markets is a great place for people-watching as well as for shopping at one of the many stalls.*

OPPOSITE *The night of nights for Sydney's gay community is the annual Gay and Lesbian Mardi Gras.*

Paddington – streets of style

Paddington, considered by many to be one of the world's best-preserved Victorian-era suburbs, is a maze of steep hillside roads lined with superbly restored terrace houses that are interspersed with art galleries, bookshops, cafes and pubs. The suburb was first settled in the early colonial days but Paddington's current look came about in the 1880s when it was subdivided for terrace house developments. After a fashionable start, the suburb suffered when bungalows on quarter-acre blocks in the outer-city suburbs became the Australian dream, and during the inter-war years Paddington degenerated into a tough slum area. However, it was rediscovered by immigrants in the 1950s, and then by young urbanites in the 1960s. Paddington has never looked back since and today it is one of Sydney's most sought-after residential postcodes.

Walk down **Oxford Street** and enjoy the many fashionable boutiques and cafes which line the street. The Uniting Church hosts Sydney's most popular Saturday bazaar, known as the **Paddington Markets**, which feature over 250 stalls (*see* Shopping) and attract crowds of shoppers including some of Sydney's most eccentric characters. On the same side of the street is the **Australian Centre for Photography** (ACP) which runs workshops and photography exhibitions. Stop at the adjoining **La Mensa** (*see* Cuisine) for coffee and nouvelle cuisine snacks or just to watch the street scene through the glass walls.

Architectural excellence

At the corner of Oxford and Ormond streets is **Juniper Hall**, Australia's oldest-surviving Georgian villa. Built in 1824 by Robert Cooper – an ex-smuggler and convict who made his fortune by distilling gin using water from the stream (which is now Cascade Street) – it is diagonally opposite the grandiose **Paddington Town Hall**. The town hall is surmounted by a 33-metre-high clock tower, built during the suburb's heyday in 1891. It is now home to the **Chauvel** cinema, which specialises in rarely seen art-house and Australian films (*see* Nightlife).

To appreciate Paddington's superb Victorian architecture, dominated by rows of pastel-coloured terrace houses decorated with ornate iron lace, wander down **Ormond Street**, where two-storey terraces continue down the steep hillside almost to the harbour. Turn left into **Glenmore Road**, then left again into **Liverpool Street**, where the curve of terrace houses with their bullnose verandahs and fanciful iron lace create a stunning architectural vista. Return to Oxford Street along Shadforth Street and directly opposite, hidden behind an impressive half-a-kilometre-long sandstone wall is the **Victoria Barracks**, a complex of Georgian-style buildings and parade grounds encompassing over 14 hectares. Each Tuesday at 10am after a solemn Changing of the Guard, the public is admitted to the barracks and its military museum for a guided tour.

Taylor Square – an epicurean culture

Continue down Oxford Street, past the eclectic bookshops, art cinemas, fashion boutiques, restaurants and cafes, to **Taylor Square** in Darlinghurst. This is the centre of Sydney's gay community, which is only rivalled in size by that of San Francisco. Every March, the Sydney Gay and Lesbian Mardi Gras (*see* Events), the city's most flamboyant and outrageous parade, is held on Oxford Street. Some night spots around Taylor Square cater exclusively for the gay crowd, but the area's many excellent restaurants and bars (*see* Cuisine and Nightlife) are extremely popular with Sydneysiders of all sexual persuasions. It is a perfect place to end up a day's tour of the Eastern Suburbs.

Useful Information

EXPLORER BUS – BONDI ROUTE

The easiest way to travel around the Eastern Suburbs is by the Explorer Bus. It begins at **Circular Quay** and stops at 20 subsequent places along the way. Passengers can get on and off at the 'Explorer' stops at any point on the trip. Buses run every 30 minutes between 9am and 6pm. An adult one-day ticket costs $20, but enquire about other easy cost-saving options including the **SydneyPass** (three, five and seven days), which can also be used on ferries, harbour cruises, and all buses (**Infoline: 131 500**).

PLACES OF INTEREST

Australian Centre for Photography: 257 Oxford Street, Paddington; open daily 11am–6pm; tel: 9332–1455.

Centennial Park: top of Oxford Street, Woollahra; open daily during daylight hours; tel: 9331–5056.

Fox Studios: Lang Road, Moore Park; Backlot open 10am–6pm daily; Bent Street open 10am–late, tel: 9383–4000, Fox Tix tel: 1300–369–849

Paddington Town Hall: 249 Oxford Street; to arrange tour, tel: 9313–0111.

Royal Randwick Racecourse: Alison Park; tel: 9663–8400.

Sacred Heart Convent: Rose Bay; visits by appointment only; tel: 9371–7144.

Sportspace Tours: for the two-hour tour of the Sydney Cricket Ground and Sydney Football Stadium, tel: 9380–0383.

St Mark's Anglican Church: Darling Point Road; open weekdays 8.30am–5pm, weekends for services; tel: 9363–3657.

Vaucluse House: Wentworth Road, Vaucluse; open daily (excl. Mon) 10am–4.30pm; $5 adult, $3 children; tel: 9388–7922.

Victoria Barracks: Oxford Street, Paddington; open Tue 9.30am–12.30pm, Military Museum open Thurs 10am–1pm, Sun 10.30am–3pm; tel: 9377–2111.

Waverley Cemetery: cnr Thomas and Trafalgar streets, Clovelly; tel: 9665–4938.

Bondi and the Eastern Suburbs

Manly and the
Northern Beaches

Day Five

MANLY AND THE NORTHERN BEACHES

Ferry to Manly • Oceanworld • Manly Corso and Beach • Northern Beaches
Barrenjoey Head • Broken Bay • Pittwater • Ku-ring-gai Chase National Park
Garigal Aboriginal Heritage Walk • Waratah Park

Ferry boats are to Sydney what cable cars are to San Francisco, and a harbour voyage is an essential experience for Sydney visitors. The most famous journey is the one from Circular Quay to Manly, and on the fifth day of our tours this is combined with a trip north from Manly along the spectacular northern beaches to Palm Beach at the tip of Barrenjoey Head. An optional return journey skirts the shores of Pittwater, travels through the Ku-ring-gai Chase National Park to a wildlife park, before heading back to the city.

Manly Ferry – the best way to see the harbour
After boarding a ferry choose a bench seat on the bow or starboard for the best views. As the ferry heads east the **Sydney Opera House** looms large on Bennelong Point, named after its famous Aboriginal resident who journeyed to England with Captain Arthur Phillip in the early colonial days. Look north to Kirribilli Point, which is crowned with two 19th-century mansions: **Admiralty House**, the city base of the Governor General, and further north, **Kirribilli House** for use by the Prime Minister. **The Royal Botanic Gardens** are on the east of the Opera House, enclosed by a stone sea wall that wraps around Farm Cove to Mrs Macquarie's Point.

A stone fort crowned by a Martello tower on the tiny rocky island will come into view. This is **Fort Denison**, dubbed Pinchgut by its convict internees because of the meagre rations. Built to house Sydney's most notorious convicts soon after

PREVIOUS PAGES *A fisherman gets an early start off the rocks at Manly, one of Sydney's most popular northern seaside resorts.*

INSET *Oceanworld near Manly Wharf is the place to see some Sydney's marine life up-close, such as stingrays and sharks.*

OPPOSITE *Palm Beach Wharf juts out into the peaceful Pittwater which is separated from the ocean by the northern peninsula.*

RIGHT *From the air it is easy to see why Freshwater and Manly's beaches are so popular with residents and visitors alike.*

BELOW *From the ferry to Manly the terraced gardens of Admiralty House, the Governor General's Sydney residence, can clearly be seen.*

the arrival of the First Fleet, Fort Denison is open for guided tours. To the east of Fort Denison is **Woolloomooloo Bay** with the Garden Island Naval Dockyard in front, and the apartment blocks of **Potts Point** behind. Luxury residences crowd the foreshores of **Elizabeth Bay**, adjacent **Rushcutters Bay**, home to the Cruising Yacht Club of Australia and around to the elite suburbs of **Darling Point**, **Double Bay**, and **Point Piper** (*see* Day 4).

On the northern foreshores are the leafy, and expensive residences of **Cremorne** and **Mosman Bay**, and the wooded promontory behind **Little Sirius Cove** shelters the wonderfully situated **Taronga Zoo** (*see* A Day at the Zoo). **Bradley's Head**, north of the zoo, was notorious for two ferry disasters earlier this century and the bays further north form part of the expansive **Sydney Harbour National Park** (*see* Harbourside Walks).

Shark Island in the middle of the harbour is popular with picnickers despite its name, and beyond is **Rose Bay**, the harbour's largest bay. This is followed by **Watsons Bay** and a number of smaller coves, and the magnificent South Head, the southern cliff at the threshold of Sydney Harbour (*see* Day 4).

When the ferry clears **Middle Head**, at the mouth of Middle Harbour, and makes its run to Manly it crosses the 1500-metre-wide entrance to Sydney Harbour where the calm waters of Port Jackson give way to the rolling swells of the Pacific Ocean. In particularly rough seas the ferry service is cancelled, but the thrill of salt spray and a knowledge that the ocean is just outside is all part of the essential Manly ferry experience. The sandstone cliff of **North Head** looms to your right as the ferry crosses the entrance, then the swells of the harbour abate as the ferry enters North Harbour and makes the short home run to **Manly Cove Wharf**.

Manly – a wedge between two waters

Sydney's founding father, Captain Arthur Phillip, thought the Aborigines were of 'manly bearing' when he first arrived in that area of the harbour and the name stuck. However, this spit of land, wedged between the harbour and the ocean, is famous not for its indigenous people, who disappeared from the area after the first colonisers arrived, but as a holiday mecca renowned for

Sydney C

Middle Head

Watsons Bay

Port Jackson

Dobroyd

Sydney Harbour National Park

North Harbour

← to North Head

Manly Cove

The Corso

Manly Beach

Pacific Ocean

Fairlight

Manly

th Steyne Beach

Queenscliff

to Northern Beaches →

Queenscliff Beach

its pine-fringed surfing beaches, funfairs, restaurants and lively atmosphere. **Manly** was developed as a resort in the 1850s by an English-born entrepreneur, H.G. Smith, who wrote 'There is no place to equal it for beauty . . . there is nothing like it in the wide, wide world'. Later, ferry companies would advertise Manly as 'Seven Miles from Sydney, a Thousand Miles from Care'. The isthmus is still a favourite holiday destination as well as a very popular residential area with close to 13 500 passengers commuting between Manly and the city's CBD daily.

After alighting at the wharf, veer left and walk around the cove, past the harbour pool on West Esplanade to **Oceanworld**. This is Australia's largest collection of marine life and visitors can watch divers handfeed giant stingrays and sharks. Oceanworld also run dive tours, including the popular 'Shark Dive Sydney' for qualified scuba divers.

If you head back towards the wharf and turn left you'll come upon **The Corso**, Manly's main street. The Corso follows an original Aboriginal trail which now links Manly Cove to the beach across the 400-metre-wide neck of the isthmus. Shops, restaurants, hotels, fun-parlours and outdoor cafes line the wide palm-lined thoroughfare. The novelist D.H. Lawrence wrote when he visited in 1922, that Manly was 'like a bit of Margate with seaside shops and restaurants, till you come out on a promenade at the end; and there is the wide Pacific rolling in on the yellow sand...' Seventy years later the vista of **Manly Beach** is still breathtaking.

A beachside promenade

A large stretch of sand runs the entire length of the coast from **Queenscliff** in the north, pass **South Steyne** and Manly beaches and around to **Shelley Beach** in the south. Surfing is excellent all along the beaches, and swimming is best

PREVIOUS PAGES *The view looking west from Manly Beach (in the foreground) to Sydney Harbour shows the extent of the Eastern and Northern Suburbs with the city in the background.*

OPPOSITE TOP *When the sun rises over Manly Beach it is usually deserted, but before long another hectic day of swimming, surfing and sunbathing will begin.*

OPPOSITE BOTTOM *Catching a few rays, feeling the warm sand between your toes, cooling off in the water, relaxing with a magazine in the shade of your beach umbrella – all this is on offer at Manly Beach.*

ABOVE *The elements pound relentlessly against the cliffs of North Head at the entrance to Sydney Harbour, creating a dramatic landscape.*

TOP *A 180-degree view of Sydney's marine life is on display in the amazing underwater tunnel, just one of the many attractions at Manly's Oceanworld.*

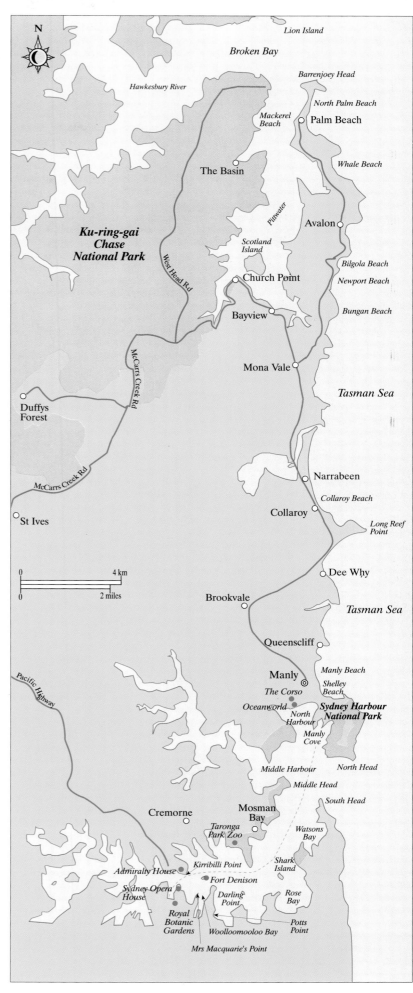

between the flags in front of the Manly Surf Life Saving Club south of The Corso. Turn left and look up to the hillside high above the beach and you will see the International College of Tourism & Hotel Management. This building was formerly St Patrick's College, a massive stone seminary with a six-storey bell tower. Drop in at the stylish **Rimini Fish Cafe** (*see* Cuisine) opposite the beach for a continental brunch or a seafood lunch.

Continue walking around the southern foreshore promenade past the little cove of **Fairy Bower** and the rock pool to sheltered Shelley Beach, popular with divers and fishermen. Follow the path up to the headland for extensive ocean views. Optional Manly walks include the scenic bushland trail to the clifftop of **North Head**, which overlooks the entrance to Sydney Harbour, and the adjacent **National Artillery Museum**. You'll need to backtrack to Bower Street and around the base of St Patrick's to Darley Road.

Heading north

Return to Manly Wharf to pick up a hire car or board the bus for the northern beaches. Bus numbers 155 or 157, running every half-hour along **Pittwater Road**, will take you to **Warringah Mall** where you can catch the Palm Beach bus, number 190, which also runs at half-hour intervals. If you have time to spare take a stroll around Warringah Mall, a huge shopping centre.

ABOVE *These century-old Norfolk Pine lining the wide white sands of Manly Beach are a distinct characteristic of Sydney's most popular beachside resort.*

OPPOSITE TOP LEFT *The green fingers of Sydney Harbour National Park on the North Head surround the old seminary above Manly Beach.*

OPPOSITE TOP RIGHT *Manly Corso links Manly Cove with the Pacific Ocean and provides an extremely colourful, busy and thoroughly entertaining throughway.*

OPPOSITE BOTTOM *Shelley Beach is a quiet little retreat in Cabbage Tree Cove at the end of a walkway from the southern end of Manly.*

The best ocean views are on the right-hand side of Pittwater Road past **Dee Why**, a long surf beach backed by a lagoon. A wildlife refuge runs north to **Long Reef** where a superb 18-hole golf course straddles the promontory. **Collaroy Beach** is next and sweeps north to **Narrabeen**, which is internationally famed for its excellent surf waves. Pittwater Road then heads away from the coast and at **Mona Vale** the bus route continues up **Barrenjoey Road** and onto what is known locally as the Peninsula, a hilly 15-kilometre-long promontory with the ocean to the east and the tranquil waters of **Pittwater**, a large saltwater inlet, to the west. Luxury residences hug both sides of the Peninsula and as the route winds up the scenic coast, real estate values climb accordingly.

Bungan Beach, next after Mona Vale, attracts surfers seeking peace and quiet as it is only accessible by a cliffside pathway. **Newport**, flanked by restaurants and fast-food shops is a favourite stopover for hungry beachgoers; the bus then climbs north, revealing wonderful ocean vistas as it winds around Bilgola Beach where wealthy beach houses line the forested cove, and finally drops down to **Avalon** with its resort-style shopping centre. Bookish travellers should take a break at **Bookocinno** (*see* Cuisine), a book store and cafe combined, renowned for its coffee and cakes and occasional pavement jazz concerts.

Past Avalon, Barrenjoey Road crosses to the western shore of the Peninsula where there are wonderful views showing the expanse of Pittwater. East of here is **Whale Beach**, with its famous wave producer, known in surfing circles as 'The Wedge', a rocky point that juts out into the ocean and creates the breakers that surfers love. Equally renowned is the restaurant/hotel **Jonahs** (*see* Cuisine), a favourite eatery of the rich and famous, with fabulous views over the beach.

OPPOSITE TOP *The famous North Narrabeen surf breaks onto the entrance of the Narrabeen Lakes, popular for surfing and water-skiing.*

OPPOSITE BOTTOM *Pittwater is a paradise for many weekend sailors who moor their boats along its waterway.*

RIGHT TOP *With the reliable onshore winds blowing in from the sea, thrill-seekers can ride the air currents above Long Reef.*

RIGHT BOTTOM *Playing the 18 holes of the Long Reef golf course is also a great way to see the best view in town as the course sits on a promontory overlooking the ocean.*

Barrenjoey Head – surrounded by water
Finally, the bus route arrives at the Peninsula's exclusive Palm Beach, home to a large slab of Sydney's 'Who's Who'. The protected southern end of the beach has a rock pool while surfing is best at **North Palm Beach**.

Across on the Pittwater side of the isthmus is a steep but short walk up to the top of Barrenjoey Head. The return walk takes around 90 minutes. Begin at the **Seaplane Wharf** on **Station Beach**. The sand dunes between the ocean and the inlet were breached by huge seas in 1974 but have now been stabilised by native plant regeneration. The trail up Barrenjoey winds past the cabbage tree palms after which Palm Beach is named, past the old harbour-master's cottage, past gnarled banksias and tea-trees and up stone steps to the 19th-century lighthouse and its ivy-covered keeper's house. A nearby grave is where the first lighthouse keeper was buried after being struck by lightning. An incomparable view of the surrounding waterways extends across Pittwater, the Pacific Ocean and **Broken Bay**, where **Lion Island**, a refuge for fairy penguins, and the **Bouddi National Park**, the beginning of the Central Coast region, reward those who venture to this northernmost tip of Sydney's coastline.

Manly and the Northern Beaches

ABOVE *Akuna Road meanders around the shores of the Coal and Candle Creek within the Ku-ring-gai Chase National Park. The park harbours over 900 native species of flora and a diversity of fauna.*

LEFT *Deep in the Ku-ring-gai Chase National Park, at the confluence of Cowan Creek and Coal and Candle Creek, lies the serene, isolated Cottage Point.*

BELOW *The expansive Pittwater provides safe moorings to craft of all shapes and sizes and comes alive at weekends when sailors take to the waters.*

Sailors ahoy!

Other exciting Palm Beach options include the ferry trip from the wharf on **Snapperman Beach** to peaceful **Mackerel Beach** and **The Basin**. Favourite destinations for yachting enthusiasts, these front the vast **Ku-ring-gai Chase National Park** on the western shores of Pittwater, and are only accessible by boat. Catamarans and sailboards are available for hire near the Palm Beach jetty, and self-chartered or skippered yachts are also on offer (*see* Cruising Sydney's Waterways). Enjoy take-away fish and chips, a Sydney tradition, in the waterfront park overlooking Pittwater at Snapperman Beach before returning to the city by bus.

National Parks – bushwalkers' haven

Those with private transport can opt for a different scenic route on the return journey. Return along Barrenjoey Road to Mona Vale and then turn right into **Pittwater Road**, which winds around the shoreline of Pittwater, described by Sydney's founding father as 'the finest piece of water I ever saw'. The road travels past the marinas of **Bayview**, crowded with yachts, to **Church Point**. Offshore is the tiny Scotland Island where there are no cars and the inhabitants use boats to commute to the mainland. From Church Point follow **McCarrs Creek Road** to enter the vast **Ku-ring-gai Chase National Park**.

For fabulous views and a range of famous bushwalks, turn left into **West Head Road**. This road continues to the end of the opposite promontory overlooking Pittwater and Palm Beach. Trails lead off to the right to **The Basin** and to the left where the flooded river valleys of **America Bay** lie on the **Hawkesbury River**. The acclaimed **Garigal Aboriginal Heritage Walk**, a 4-kilometre loop walk that embraces Aboriginal engraving sites, rainforest, heathland and beaches, begins at the Garigal Picnic Area.

Back on McCarrs Creek Road, the route continues through sandstone bushland, characteristic of how Sydney looked before the coming of the Europeans, to emerge at **Terrey Hills**. At the roundabout before Mona Vale Road, turn left into **Booralie Road** and continue through **Duffys Forest** following the signs to the **Waratah Park**, a private wildlife sanctuary where the world-famous television series 'Skippy' was filmed. (Waratah Park is also accessible by **Forest Coach Lines** bus number 284 from **Chatswood** railway station.) Apart from kangaroos the park also houses koalas and other unique Aussie animals, including Tasmanian Devils.

Return to the city via Mona Vale Road through exclusive **St Ives** and then turn left onto the **Pacific Highway** at **Gordon** and follow the signs to the Harbour Bridge and the city.

Useful Information

GETTING THERE

The **Manly Ferry** and the **JetCats** depart from wharves 2 and 3 at **Circular Quay** every half-hour throughout the day. The JetCat is twice as fast (15 minutes) as the ferry, but lacks the tradition and ambience. Travellers intending to explore further on up the northern beaches from **Manly** should purchase a **Bus/Ferry Day Tripper** ticket ($12 return), which is easier and cheaper than buying tickets along the way. Another option, which will allow you to continue on into the national parks, is to hire a car, which is also the optimum way to tour the northern beaches. Car hire is available in Manly at **Manly Car Rentals** (tel: 9948–4516) or Hurst Rentals (tel: 9948–3010). If you organise before the day you can pick the car up on your arrival at Manly.

PLACES OF INTEREST

Bookocinno: 37a Old Barrenjoey Road, Avalon; tel: 9973–1244.

Fort Denison: Sydney Harbour; daily tours from Circular Quay; tel: 9247–5033.

Garigal Aboriginal Heritage Walk: see Ku-ring-gai Chase National Park.

Ku-ring-gai Chase National Park: Bobbin Head, Turramurra; open daily; tel: 9457–9322 (Mon–Fri) or 9457–9310 (weekends).

National Artillery Museum: Scenic Drive, Manly; open Wed, Sat, Sun noon–4pm; tel: 9976–1138.

Oceanworld: West Esplanade, Manly; open daily; 10am–5.30pm; tel: 9949–2644.

Shark Island: Sydney Harbour; prior bookings necessary; tel: 9337–5511.

Waratah Park: Namba Road, Duffys Forest; open daily 10am–5pm; tel: 9450–2377.

Palm Beach Experience organises day tours of the Peninsula's northern point, which combine a range of activities including a guided bushwalk in the national park, a visit to Aboriginal rock engravings and Palm Beach, viewing Pittwater by boat, and a picnic-style lunch; tel: 9974–1096 for further information and bookings.

ABOVE LEFT *A uniquely Australian road sign warns motorists to be careful of wildlife out for a stroll.*

Manly and the Northern Beaches

Exploring the
Western Harbour

Day Six

Exploring the Western Harbour

Balmain • Waterman's Cottage • Yurulbin • Parramatta River • Drummoyne Foreshore Walkway
Homebush Bay • Sydney Olympic Park • Parramatta • Elizabeth Farm
Old Government House • Parramatta Park

The pleasant trip by RiverCat (an express catamaran) through the western harbour and then upriver to Parramatta, Australia's second oldest city, can be done as a leisurely all-day tour, or for more energetic travellers it can be combined with a short ferry ride and a morning stroll through the historic suburb of Balmain. Both trips begin and end at Circular Quay ferry terminal.

Balmain – an historic stroll

There is a lot to explore in **Balmain** with plenty of good cafes for breakfast/brunch or morning tea. Ferries pass under the Harbour Bridge, stop at **Milsons Point** and **McMahons Point**, and then pass the historic finger wharves of **Walsh Bay** and head across to **Darling Street Wharf** at the eastern end of the Balmain peninsula. Alight here and read the notice board by the roadside at **Thornton Park** on your right, which gives details of the **Balmain History Trail**. This trail was inspired by Balmain's most famous resident, **Dawn Fraser**, the swimming star who won gold medals at the three Olympics between 1956 and 1964. The following walk is a shortened version, but maps and information on the entire trail can be picked up from the **Balmain Watch House** (*see* page 93) on Saturday afternoons.

The suburb of Balmain has had a chequered history. It originated as a fashionable residential area, but after a shipyard was constructed it became a working-class suburb renowned for its fiery unionists, pubs on every corner, and its

PREVIOUS PAGES *The magnificent curve of the Gladesville Bridge vaults the Parramatta River and provides a vital link between the city's north-western suburbs and its centre.*

INSET *McMahons Point ferry wharf is just around the corner from Lavender Bay, and provides a convenient commuter terminus for the suburb's residents.*

OPPOSITE *The sleek RiverCat provides one of the most scenic journeys to and from the city to Parramatta, the demographic heart of Sydney.*

ABOVE *Houses at McMahons Point face the pretty inlet of Lavender Bay, just west of the Sydney Harbour Bridge on the northern shore.*

BELOW *Ferries connect many parts of the harbour, and wharves like McMahons Point allow commuters easy access to Circular Quay.*

North Sydney

Sydney Harbour B

Lane Cove River

Woolwich

Hunters Hill

Wrights Point

Gladesville Bridge

to Parramatta

Parramatta River

Huntleys Point

Sydney CBD

Sydney Tower

Cockatoo Island

Snapper and Spectacle islands

Victoria Road

Drummoyne

Five Dock Bay

Five Dock Point

ABOVE *Balmain has been rejuvenated over the last 25 years, with older homes being prized by people wanting to live near the city.*

PREVIOUS PAGES *Heading west from the city centre, the harbour becomes the Parramatta River as the expanse of water passes Cockatoo Island and flows under the arch of the Gladesville Bridge.*

OPPOSITE *Darling Street, the main thoroughfare of harbourside Balmain, is lined with trendy shops and eateries.*

BELOW *Gentrified, renovated and repainted, the old working-class cottages of Balmain have been given a new lease on life, as have the shops and eateries that help give the suburb its village ambience.*

independent and outspoken residents. Balmain was rediscovered in the 1960s and, after the relocation of its shipyards and many of its industries, it revamped itself once again into an upmarket residential neighbourhood.

Historic architecture

Walk up the hill on **Darling Street**, past the old sandstone **Waterman's Cottage** (1841) on the right, which once belonged to the oarsman who rowed passengers across to Sydney before the days of motorised ferries. Opposite, on the left, is the former seamen's pub, the **Shipwrights Arms** (1846). Continue up Darling Street and enjoy the 19th-century architecture en route, taking a look on the right, down leafy **Duke Street** lined with Balmain terrace houses.

Darling Street then runs downhill from Duke Street, past the **Balmain Bowling Club** on the left, and then up again past the **Balmain Watch House**, built in 1854, on the same side. The historic and very popular **London Hotel** is next, then **Gladstone Park**, full of lawns and attractive flower beds.

Next door is **St Andrew's Congregational Church**, the venue of the very popular **Balmain Markets** held every Saturday (*see* Events). Along this busy stretch of Darling Street there is a concentration of bookshops, gift shops and eateries; a good place to stop for a hearty breakfast or brunch is at **Omnivore**, a bustling pavement cafe that's steeped in village atmosphere (*see* Cuisine).

Head back to McDonald Street, opposite the park, and walk downhill and along **Thames Street**. Turn left into Trouton Street, past the old **Forth and Clyde Hotel** (now offices) for **Mort Bay Park**. Until 1959 this area housed the workers for the nearby docklands, but when the shipyards and docks were relocated, it was revived by suburban middle-class families who rediscovered inner-city living. Continue along **Cameron Street**, and turn right into **Grove Street** for **Birchgrove Park**. Turn left along the waterfront pathway for peaceful **Snails Bay**, lined with boatsheds, and climb the stairs to turn right into **Louisa Road**, which straddles the ridge of a thin promontory jutting out into the harbour. The exclusive residences on either side of the road all have million-dollar harbour views. Walk to the tip of the point where **Yurulbin Park** is situated at the far end and catch the ferry from the wharf back to Circular Quay.

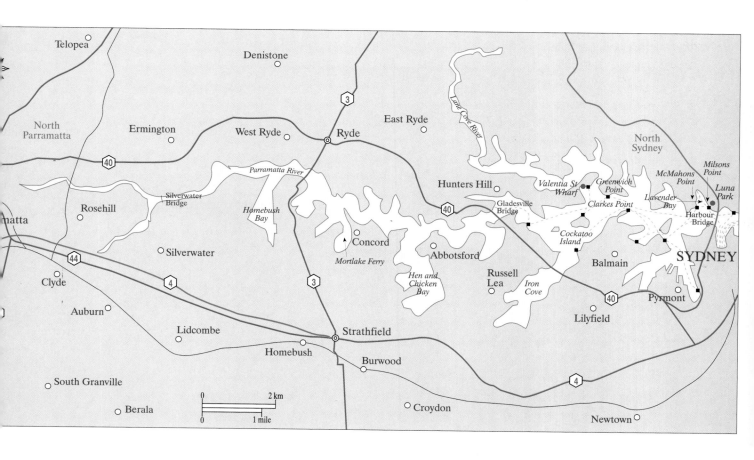

Heading upharbour

The RiverCat which travels upharbour to Parramatta has become one of the most popular ferry trips. The waters churn white as it reverses out of Circular Quay and then swings around under the **Sydney Harbour Bridge**. Look up as it does so to appreciate the dimensions of this superb engineering feat. First stop is on the northern foreshore, **Milsons Point** beside the huge grinning face of **Luna Park**, which was once Australia's best-known fun fair. The next stop, just across picturesque

Lavender Bay, is **McMahons Point**, where the waterside **Sails Restaurant** (*see* Cuisine) tempts lunch-goers with its seafood and fabulous harbour views. The RiverCat rounds **Blues Point** to starboard and then heads south to **Yurulbin Point**, the end of the Balmain walk.

Lane Cove River enters the harbour on the northern side between **Greenwich Point** and **Clarkes Point Reserve**, where fishermen try their luck. Leafy and historic **Hunters Hill** sprawls across the long promontory on the northern foreshores. This prestigious suburb, renowned for its tree-lined streets, magnificent gardens and homes, offers interesting walks for visitors who appreciate grand 19th-century residences, and is the start of the 14-day **Great North Walk**, which takes in all the national parks between Sydney and Newcastle. Hunters Hill is also served by a ferry which travels between **Valentia Street Wharf** and Circular Quay.

Parramatta River – a passage west

The western waterway now becomes the **Parramatta River** as the RiverCat passes under the concrete arch of the **Gladesville Bridge** before it stops to let off commuters at **Gladesville Wharf** on the northern foreshores. At **Abbotsford**, to the south, on the shores of superbly named **Hen and Chicken Bay**, is the **Sydney Rowing Club** with a popular restaurant which is open to the public. RiverCats stop at Abbotsford at irregular intervals, so check times first.

From Abbotsford there are enjoyable short waterfront walks or, for energetic visitors, there is the 16-kilometre **Drummoyne Foreshore Walkway** which was completed for Australia's bicentenary in 1988.

The foreshores flatten out as the RiverCat heads west. Watch out for the **Mortlake Ferry**, one of Sydney's few remaining car ferries; it runs from Mortlake to **Putney Point**. South from here is the old convalescent hospital at **Concord**, which has a stone clock tower and an old-style decorative jetty. More commuters jump off at **Meadowbank** just past the **Concord Bridge**.

Homebush Bay, the site for the 2000 Olympics, is the next place to look out for along this route. Formerly industrial land, Homebush Bay has been reinvented. Eight hundred hectares have been transformed into a magnificent sporting complex of stadiums, parklands and athletic centres, including an international aquatic centre, the giant Stadium Australia, residential complexes and a connecting railway. The site is also home to the new Sydney Showground, where the famous Royal Easter Show is held.

Adjacent to the sporting complex is **Bicentennial Park**, a 90-hectare parkland of indigenous trees and shrubs. A 5-kilometre long board-walk winds through extensive mangrove forests that cover approximately 50 hectares of wetlands.

OPPOSITE TOP *The fantastically grotesque entrance to Luna Park lights up at night, little changed in appear-ance since its opening in 1935.*

OPPOSITE BOTTOM *The simple design of the Gladesville Bridge belies the fact that it supports one of Sydney's busiest arteries, Victoria Road.*

ABOVE *Purpose built as the main venue for the 2000 Olympic Games, Stadium Australia is the largest outdoor venue in Olympic history and was designed specifically for the Australian climate.*

RIGHT *The brand-new, ultra-modern swimming centre at the Homebush Bay sporting complex, built in preparation for the 2000 Olympics.*

Exploring the Western Harbour

Further down river is **Meadowbank** where the mangroves close in as the river narrows and the RiverCat slows down for the final run up to Parramatta's **Charles Street Wharf**. Check the RiverCat's return times before you wander off to explore Parramatta.

Parramatta – the head of the river

Climb the stairs to the corner of Charles and Phillip streets, and if you're in need of refreshment pop into **Cranks Cafe** (Free Cuisine), which overlooks the jetty and specialises in vegetarian snacks and herbal teas as well as regular fare like cakes and coffee. **Parramatta** was first discovered by Europeans only three months after Sydney was founded in 1788. The land along the river flats was sought after for agriculture as the rocky foreshores of the harbour were unsuitable for farming. Australia's first crops of wheat, barley and maize were harvested within 12 months and 'The Cradle City' is where the nation's first orchard,

vineyard, winery and brewery were established. The name Parramatta is an Aboriginal word whose meaning is thought to be either, appropriately, 'head of the river' or the more obscure 'place where eels lie down'.

Original homesteads

The easiest way to appreciate all the city's sights is to hop on board the **Parramatta Explorer** bus. First stop is at 70 Alice Street, **Elizabeth Farm**. Built in 1793, it is reputed to be the nation's oldest building and the forerunner of the Australian homestead with its large shady roof and deep verandahs. Surrounded by a recreated garden from the 1830s, it was originally built by John and Elizabeth Macarthur – pioneers of the Australian merino sheep industry. The interiors have been faithfully preserved in the early 19th-century period, and visitors can relax and enjoy the historical ambience while partaking of Devonshire tea or lunch at the tearooms.

OPPOSITE *Slithering like a snake out into the Parramatta River, Drummoyne is drenched in sunlight, with the suburbs of Balmain and Lilyfield in the background.*

BELOW *Historic Elizabeth Farm at Parramatta, the home of Australia's pioneering merino sheep industry, has provided the architectural inspiration for many Australian homes.*

The bus also stops at the superbly restored **Hambledon Cottage** on Hassall Street, where Penelope Lucas, the governess of the Macarthurs' children, once resided. When John Macarthur was sent back to England to be court-martialled for plotting against the governor (he was later acquitted and returned to the colony), Penelope helped Elizabeth Macarthur with the successful running of Elizabeth Farm. The oak, cork and olive trees, which still surround the cottage, were planted over a century and a half ago.

Experiment Farm Cottage, the next stop on Ruse Street, is a charming Indian-style bungalow dating from the 1830s which stands on the site of the first land grant made in Australia in 1789 to James Ruse, an emancipated convict. The farm, where grain was first grown successfully, was initially mooted as an 'experiment' by Sydney's founding father, Governor Phillip.

ABOVE *Old Government House, one of Parramatta's several historic buildings, w̶ the original Governor's residence, but can now be hired for functions and is als̶ open to the public for inspection.*

Old Government House – a country residence

The Explorer then heads for historic **St Patrick's Cemetery** on the corner of Church Street and Pennant Hills Road, and then to **Old Government House** in Parramatta Park. This elegant two-storey Georgian building was the country residence of the NSW governors until the 1850s, and now houses a fine collection of early colonial furniture. It is reputed to be the oldest public building in Australia. **Parramatta Park**, the surrounding parklands, were once known as the Governor's Domain and they contain other historical buildings including the nation's first observatory. The park is a favourite picnic spot for local residents and a venue for bike riding, boating and hot-air ballooning. For details, enquire at the **Parramatta Visitors Centre**.

The last stop before the Explorer returns to the wharf is **Parramatta Leagues Club**, home to the city's rugby league team. The club's facilities include a huge gaming lounge and two restaurants, which are open to visitors. If you haven't been inside an Aussie-style club this is a good opportunity to witness the 'untourist' side of Parramatta and try your luck on the poker machines. A shuttle-bus also connects back to the RiverCat wharf from the club.

Return to the city on the RiverCat or, if you miss the last ferry at 6.35pm, there is a regular train service from Parramatta Railway Station to the city.

OPPOSITE BOTTOM *The Indian-style bungalow of Parramatta's Experimental Farm is one the city's remaining tangible links with its agricultural past.*

ABOVE *Hambledon Cottage is surrounded by 150-year-old oak, cork and olive trees and has the wide verandahs of the classic Australian-colonial style.*

Useful Information

GETTING THERE AND AROUND

Ferries leave for **Balmain** every half hour from **Wharf No 5** at **Circular Quay**. The 10-minute journey will cost $2.80 for adults. For **Parramatta**, the **RiverCat** leaves from **Wharf No 5** between 7.50am and 6.45pm (the last return from Parramatta is at 7.55pm). Times vary throughout the day. The journey takes around one hour and if it's a sunny day the best view is from the benches on the bow. Passengers can buy a single ticket at each end: adults $4.80 and children $2.40.

From **Charles Street Wharf** at Parramatta the easiest way to appreciate all the sights is to catch the **Parramatta Explorer Bus**. It meets each ferry and departs from the top of the wharf steps. The tour takes around one hour to circumnavigate the city, but passengers can alight at any of the stops and reboard at any time on one of the following buses.

HOMEBUSH BAY

Bus tours of the Olympic site leave the Homebush Information Centre on Herb Elliot Avenue every 30 minutes 10am–2pm; $5 adults, $2.50 children. The **Sydney Aquatic Centre** has a spectacular underwater viewing platform in the competition pool, and a leisure area with water slides, artificial rapids and spa pools. Tours run at 10am, 12pm, and 2pm; $12 adults, $8 children; tel: 9752–3666. Sydney Ferries run ferry and bus tours of the site from Wharf 5 at Circular Quay; $15 adults and children. Visitors can also make their own way to the **Olympic Park** by buses, which leave Strathfield Railway Station from 9.30am. Phone 9714–7888 for further information.

PLACES OF INTEREST

Balmain Watch House: 179 Darling Street; open Sat and Sun 12pm–3pm.
Elizabeth Farm: open daily 10am–5pm; $6 adult, $3 child; $15 family; tel: 9635–9488.
Experiment Farm Cottage: open Tue–Thu 10am–4pm, Sun 11am–4pm; $5 adults, $3 children, $12 family; tel: 9635–5655.
Hambledon Cottage: open Wed, Thu, Sat and Sun 11am–4pm; $3 adults, $2 children; tel: 9635–6924.
Old Government House: Parramatta Park; open Mon–Fri 10am–4pm, Sat–Sun 11am–4pm; $6 adults, $4 children, $12 family; tel: 9635–8149.
Parramatta Leagues Club: 15 O'Connell Street; tel: 9683–1888.
Parramatta Visitors Centre: Church and Market streets; open Mon–Fri 10am–5pm, Sat–Sun and public holidays 10am–4pm; tel: 9630–3703.

West to the
Blue Mountains

Day Seven

WEST TO THE BLUE MOUNTAINS

Australia's Wonderland • Norman Lindsay's House • Wentworth Falls
Jamison Valley • Leura • Katoomba • Three Sisters • Hydro Majestic Hotel • Grose Valley
Mount Tomah Botanic Garden • Richmond • Windsor

nown as the **Grand Circular Drive**, this day tour heads approximately 100 kilometres west from the city along the Great Western Highway to the scenic Blue Mountains and returns via The Bells Line of Road and the historic Macquarie towns of Richmond and Windsor. There are so many attractions in the mountains that many travellers may wish to extend their stay, particularly if they want to embark on one of the area's several famous bushwalks. Accommodation is plentiful and ranges from majestic old-style hotels to 'bed and breakfast' establishments in historic homes with idyllic bushland retreats.

The route to the west

By car, begin at Circular Quay and head south on **George Street**, which turns into Broadway at **Central Railway Station** and then becomes **Parramatta Road** (also known as the **Great Western Highway**) as the road passes **Sydney University**. At Strathfield turn onto the **Western Motorway** (M4) which affords an easier route west than the notorious Parramatta Road.

Australia's Wonderland – a family treat

At **Eastern Creek** travellers with children might like to make a detour to **Australia's Wonderland**, the nation's largest theme park. Within the park

PREVIOUS PAGES   *The renowned rock formation, the Three Sisters, rises up majestically from the forested valley at Katoomba in the Blue Mountains, west of Sydney.*

INSET   *The popular Echo Point Lookout draws visitors from all over the world to see the Three Sisters standing sentinel alongside the sweeping Jamison Valley.*

OPPOSITE *The sheer-sided sandstone walls of the vast Grose Valley in the Blue Mountains were cut by the Grose River.*

ABOVE *A bridge connects across to the first of the Three Sisters at the end of the Giant Stairway.*

West to the Blue Mountains

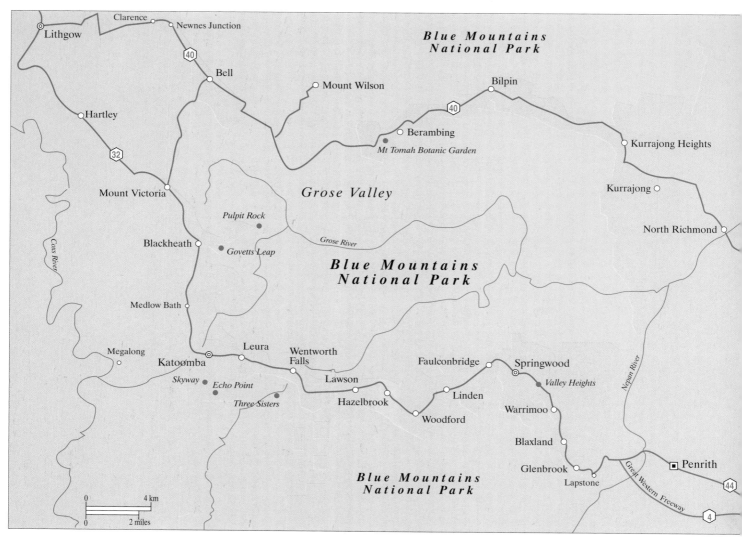

Lithgow · Clarence · Newnes Junction · *Blue Mountains National Park* · 40 · Bell · Mount Wilson · Bilpin · 40 · Berambing · Kurrajong Heights · Hartley · 32 · *Mt Tomah Botanic Garden* · Kurrajong · *Grose Valley* · North Richmond · Mount Victoria · *Pulpit Rock* · Blackheath · *Grose River* · *Govetts Leap* · **Blue Mountains National Park** · *Cass River* · Medlow Bath · Megalong · Leura · Wentworth Falls · Faulconbridge · Springwood · Katoomba · *Valley Heights* · *Skyway* · *Echo Point* · Lawson · Linden · Warrimoo · *Three Sisters* · Hazelbrook · Woodford · Blaxland · *Nepean River* · Glenbrook · Penrith · Lapstone · *Great Western Freeway* · 44 · 4 · **Blue Mountains National Park**

0 — 4 km
0 — 2 miles

OPPOSITE *Like the rings of an ancient tree, the sandstone cliffs that border the Jamison Valley, when seen from the Three Sisters, present a giant tableau of the natural history of the Blue Mountains.*

ABOVE *The awe-inspiring panorama of the Grose Valley in the Blue Mountains drops away to the foothills of the Great Dividing Range and allows visitors to contemplate the forces of nature.*

---

are a number of sections based on themes like a cartoon-inspired 'land', a wildlife park, a goldrush village, a 'beach' with water slides, and a fun fair with the fastest roller-coaster ride in the Southern Hemisphere. You could easily spend a whole day at Australia's Wonderland, or just an hour.

The Blue Mountains – an inland gateway

Continue along the M4 to **Penrith** where the motorway crosses the **Nepean River**. The rowing events for the 2000 Olympic Games will be held on this river. After this point, the motorway merges back into the **Great Western Highway** and the road climbs up the first ridge of the **Blue Mountains**. The road makes it hard to imagine that the range was once considered impassable. The explorers Blaxland, Wentworth and Lawson, whose names are immortalised by mountain townships, made the first crossing by Europeans in 1813. The mountains, actually a sandstone plateau bisected by deep gorges, are named after their distinctive colouring caused by a blue haze created when light filters through the mist of oil discharged from the eucalyptus forests.

The highway through the mountains parallels the railway line, which follows the main ridge, and the townships cluster on the heights leaving the vast forested canyons, which drop off at either side, to their uninhabited splendour. The towns en route include **Lapstone**, **Glenbrook**, **Blaxland**, **Warrimoo** and **Valley Heights**.

West to the Blue Mountains

Norman Lindsay Gallery and Museum – an artist's sanctuary

At the pleasant village of **Springwood** continue along the highway and turn right at Grose Road for the **Norman Lindsay Gallery and Museum** (it is clearly signposted), housed in the former home and studio of one of Australia's most versatile and controversial artists. Famed for his paintings of nudes and satyrs, his popular children's books, his dislike of the bourgeoisie and his bohemian lifestyle, Lindsay resided here for 60 years until his death in 1969. Sam Neill played the famous artist in *Sirens*, a movie which also starred the Australian supermodel Elle Macpherson. The property is now owned by the National Trust and on display are Lindsay's paintings, drawings and exquisite model ships; the surrounding wisteria-draped gardens contain many of his sculptures.

Jamison Valley – splendid views

Continue along the Great Western Highway past the town of **Faulconbridge** which is famed for its former resident Sir Henry Parkes. (Parkes was the 'Father of Australian Federation' and his grave is in the town's cemetery.) Further on, past the small towns of **Linden**, **Hazelbrook** and **Lawson**, you'll come to **Wentworth Falls**. You'll need to turn left into Falls Road from the highway and continue until the road ends at **Falls Reserve**, a pleasant picnic area and lookout at the top of the cliffs overlooking the spectacular **Jamison Valley** and the 300-metre-high falls.

Walks radiate from the reserve, including the renowned **National Pass Trail** which follows a natural rock ledge halfway down the cliff face with excellent views of some of the region's most spectacular scenery. Bushwalkers can walk along the clifftop to the **Valley of the Waters Reserve** (which is also accessible by car on Fletcher Street off Falls Road) and from there the descent passes the delightful **Empress Falls**, through the beautiful Valley of the Waters, past rainforests and under waterfalls as it winds around the National Pass and then ascends onto a stone staircase

OPPOSITE TOP *The home of the bohemian artist Norman Lindsay at Springwood is now a gallery and museum displaying the artist's work and was the location for the film about him, Sirens.*

OPPOSITE BOTTOM *The nude female form was one of Lindsay's favourite subjects and it is exemplified by this sculpture located in the expansive gardens of his Springwood home.*

ABOVE *A symphony of bush sights and sounds mingle at the Valley of the Waters, where water cascades down the rock face of the Jamison Valley while stately gums surround its path.*

West to the Blue Mountains

beside the plunging **Wentworth Falls**. The views are staggering and the entire 6-kilometre trail takes around three hours to complete.

For a quicker walk to the falls, and a chance to visit one of the mountains' most famous historical homes, turn left onto **Yester Road**, before the town of Wentworth Falls, and continue to the end for **Yestergrange**. This wonderful country retreat is renowned not only for its gardens and views, but for an amazing collection of Victorian memorabilia. It was built in 1886 for a retired sea captain, then later became the residence of a former state premier. The bushwalk to the falls starts from the grounds of Yestergrange but for less energetic visitors the Devonshire teas served in a glass-sided tearoom overlooking the gardens may sound more appealing.

For another spectacular view, go back to the highway, continue west but before the quaint old-style town of **Leura** turn left into Scott Avenue, then left again on Gladstone Road, right on Fitzroy Street, left into Watkins Road, and left · again along Sublime Point Road. Possibly the mountains' most impressive lookout is situated at the end of this road and the views from the aptly-named **Sublime Point Lookout** pan across the Jamison Valley, surrounded by vertical sandstone cliffs, to the **Three Sisters** at **Katoomba** (*see* later, this tour) and beyond.

A piece of yore

Back on Fitzroy Street, turn left at the end into Everglades Avenue for the National Trust property of the same name. Dating from the 1930s, the lush **Everglades Gardens** are at their glorious best during the spring and autumn months. Continue on down Everglades Street to Railway Parade for the **Leura Village Mall**. This atmospheric stretch recalls the style of the 1920s; here cafes and restaurants (*see* Cuisine) compete with galleries, gift shops and boutiques.

After stopping for a browse, drive down The Mall and turn right into Gordon Road. This is where the famous **Cliff Drive** begins winding spectacularly around the top of the escarpment connecting the village of Leura to Katoomba. Along the way stop and enjoy the **Leura Cascades** and **Honeymoon Lookout**.

OPPOSITE TOP *Katoomba has been a resort town for Sydneysiders escaping the summer heat for over 100 years.*

OPPOSITE BOTTOM *Sculpture abounds in the Everglade Gardens.*

RIGHT *The spectacular Wentworth Falls plunge down the cliff edge to seemingly disappear into the chasms of the earth.*

BELOW *The Post Office at Wentworth Falls exemplifies the Australian Federation-style architecture.*

BOTTOM *Moss and lichen thrive on the cool, damp steps carved into the sandstone at the Everglades Gardens.*

The Three Sisters – majestic siblings

Before the main street of Katoomba is **Echo Point**, the most famous of the mountains' viewpoints. It overlooks the renowned rock formation, the **Three Sisters**, siblings turned to stone according to an Aboriginal legend, rising from the escarpment in their regal glory. Below you can clearly see the massive box canyons that thwarted many early exploration attempts with their rainforested gullies backed by vertical cliffs. Around Echo Point there are dozens of bushwalks and at the nearby **Blue Mountains Information Centre** visitors can buy maps of the trails as well as souvenirs. Accommodation can also be arranged at the information centre.

For visitors on a tight schedule the best bushwalk is the easy 1-kilometre-return Three Sisters Walk around the clifftop from Echo Point. For travellers intending to stay over-night, the best walk is most probably the 5-kilometre circuit which descends the **Giant Stairway** beside the Three Sisters to the bottom of the valley and then winds through the lush rainforest and past waterfalls along the **Federal Pass Trail** to the foot of the **Scenic Railway**. This near vertical train track, reputed to be the world's steepest railway, was originally built in 1885 to transport coal and miners. If you don't walk the trail you can still catch the steep ride from the clifftop to the valley floor and back again. Head down Cliff Drive to the start of the railway, west of Echo Point. Adjacent to the Scenic Railway is the **Skyway**, a cable car that traverses a corner of the Jamison Valley offering wonderful views of the valley and the **Katoomba Falls**, which plunge down the escarpment.

Katoomba has been a very popular holiday resort for over a century and boasts lovely Victorian and Edwardian guesthouses and residences. Treat yourself with a visit to the heritage-listed **Paragon Cafe** (*see* Cuisine), which still retains its unique Art Deco interior and is famous for its excellent handmade chocolates. For dining style and enjoyment of the world-famed views, try **Lilians** (*see* Cuisine) at Lilianfels Avenue.

For health and relaxation

From Katoomba take the Cliff Drive west past **Cahill's Lookout** with its grand views of **Megalong Valley** and back along Narrow Neck Road and Valley Road to the Great Western Highway. Turn left for the hamlet of **Medlow Bath**, 6 kilometres west, with its renowned **Hydro Majestic Hotel**, built as a health resort in the late 19th-century. Looking like a transplant from the French Riviera, this Edwardian-style hotel affords fabulous views over the Megalong Valley. Sit back in the casino lounge and enjoy the ambience of a bygone era and an incredible view.

Continue west for **Blackheath** which is famed for its beautiful rhododendron gardens and spectacular views across the **Grose Valley** to the north of town. **Govetts Leap Road** leads to the viewpoint of the same name, which offers an expansive panorama of the northern valleys of the Blue Mountains National Park. A number of popular bushwalks begin here at the adjacent **National Parks and Wildlife Service Heritage Centre** including the one-hour-return **Fairfax Heritage Track**, built specially for people in wheelchairs. Other walks include the 90-minute-return walk to **Pulpit Rock**, the four-hour circuit through the **Grand Canyon**, and the eight-hour walk through the enchanting **Blue Gum Forest**. If you are thinking of staying the night, the gracious guesthouse **Cleopatra's** on the street of the same name is an elegant Victorian retreat with wonderful gardens, famed for its nouvelle cuisine (*see* Cuisine).

Top *The archway entrance to the Giant Stairway marks the beginning of the walk to the Three Sisters.*

Bottom left *The Giant Stairway winds its way down the cliff, offering many scenic vantage points along the way.*

Bottom right *Inside the famous Hydro Majestic Hotel at Medlow Bath the stately lounge room allows unbelievable views across the Megalong Valley.*

West to the Blue Mountains

Mountain gardens

Continue west from Blackheath to the historical settlement of **Mount Victoria**, well known for its heritage pubs and Victorian-era architecture. Turn left here and continue along the Darling Causeway to the **Bells Line of Road** and then turn right. On the left, 7 kilometres along, is the turnoff for **Mount Wilson**, an historic wealthy retreat famed for its gardens and avenues lined with deciduous European trees which are at their best in autumn. Patrick White, Australia's Nobel Prize-winning novelist, stayed here during his youth and wrote about the region in *Flaws in the Glass*. This delightful village is well worth a visit, especially during spring and autumn when colour abounds.

Continue along the Bells Line of Road for **Mount Tomah Botanic Garden**, the cool climate gardens of the Royal Botanic Gardens, with their special conifer and rhododendron collections and their views from the 1000-metre-high mountaintop location.

To the Hawkesbury Valley

Past **Bilpin**, a well-known apple-producing region where roadside stalls offer good-quality bargains, is **Kurrajong Heights**. From here on a clear day you can see all the way back to Sydney. The antique shops and arts and crafts galleries at Kurrajong Heights are great for browsing, or alternatively detour to Kurrajong village on the **Old Bells Line of Road**, which also offers tea rooms and excellent handicraft shops.

From Kurrajong the main road drops from the plateau down to the plains, crosses the flood plains of the Nepean River and arrives at **Richmond**, one of the oldest towns in the Hawkesbury Valley. First settled in 1794, Richmond became a prosperous market town in the 19th century and many historical buildings still survive. In Windsor Street (turn left from Kurrajong Road at Richmond Park and then right) there are a number of grand residences which were built in the mid-19th century.

Continue along Windsor Street out of town, past the airfields of the **Richmond RAAF Base** on your left and the **Hawkesbury Racecourse** on your right to **Windsor**, the most famous of the five Hawkesbury Valley towns. Windsor was established by Governor Lachlan Macquarie in the early 19th century. It is well worth wandering through, and maps of its profuse historic sights can be obtained at the **Hawkesbury Museum and Tourist Centre** in Thompson Square (left into George Street and continue till the end). Windsor's best known building is **St Matthew's Anglican Church** with its great square tower built by the famous ex-convict architect Francis Greenway between 1817 and 1820. Also designed by him is the sandstone courthouse built in 1822. Another important building is the **John Tebbutt Observatory**, which is still owned by the original family on the street of the same name.

From Windsor, motorists can return to Sydney via the Windsor Road to Parramatta and then follow the M4 motorway and the Great Western Highway back to the city.

ABOVE Along the cliff face of the escarpment, the sun illuminates the gums that produce the eucalyptus oil responsible for creating the blue haze that gave the area and the mountains their name.

OPPOSITE The Grand Canyon is a spectacular section of the walk down into the Grose Valley. Much of the surrounding bush is in an almost primeval condition.

Useful Information

GETTING THERE

Private transport is essential to view the sights along the way to the **Blue Mountains**. The main advantage, of course, is that you can travel at your own pace. There are many car hire firms which will deliver a car directly to your hotel. Alternatively **CityRail** trains run regularly from **Central Railway Station** to **Katoomba**, the 'capital' of the Blue Mountains. **The Blue Mountains Explorer Bus** departs from Katoomba Station every hour and visits 26 different sights; passengers can alight as often as they like and pick up another bus later on for the same fixed price. Many bus companies also offer daytrip tours to the Blue Mountains. Check with any visitor information booth for details.

PLACES OF INTEREST

Australia's Wonderland: Wallgrove Road, Eastern Creek (35-minute drive from city); open daily 10am–5pm; $39 adults, $27 children aged 4–12 (unlimited rides all day); tel: 9830–9100.

Blue Mountains Information Centre: tel: 4739–6266.

Everglades Gardens: Everglades Avenue, Leura; open daily 10am–5pm in spring and summer; 10am–4pm in winter and autumn; $6 adults, $4 students, $2 children; tel: 4784–1938.

Hawkesbury Museum and Tourist Centre: tel: 4577–2310.

Hydro Majestic Hotel: Medlow Bath; tel: 4788–1002.

John Tebbutt Observatory: tel: 4577–2485.

Mount Tomah Botanic Gardens: tel: 4567–2154.

National Parks and Wildlife Service Heritage Centre: tel: 4787–8877.

Norman Lindsay Gallery and Museum: Grose Road; open daily (excl. Tues) 11am–5pm; $5 adults, $2.50 students, $1 children; tel: 4741–1067.

Paragon Cafe: Katoomba; tel: 4782–2928.

Scenic Railway: Cliff Drive, Katoomba; tel: 4782–2699.

Skyway: Cliff Drive, Katoomba; open daily 9am–5pm; $4 (single) $7 (return) adults, $2 (single and return) children; tel: 4782–2699.

St Matthew's Anglican Church: tel: 4577–3073.

113

West to the Blue Mountains

A Day at the Zoo

Special Itinerary

A DAY AT THE ZOO

Consistently voted to be the most spectacular zoo in the world, Sydney's **Taronga Zoo** takes its name from the Aboriginal word for 'beautiful harbour view', a description obvious to any visitor. Located on the northern harbour foreshores above **Athol Bay** and the heights of **Bradleys Head**, the zoo not only affords some of the city's best views, but offers the visitor a fascinating introduction to Australia's unique wildlife and a diverse spectrum of animals, birds and reptiles from around the world.

Moving the ark

Taronga Zoo has been in existence since 1916 when the animals were moved from the former site at **Moore Park**. Sydneysiders turned out in their numbers to watch the spectacular operation, worthy of Noah, when 177 mammals, including Jessie the elephant, and 329 birds were transported, without incident, across the harbour by vehicular ferry. Most of the zoo's early constructions from the 'concrete era' have been upgraded and now the animals are exhibited in more attractive, natural and spacious surroundings. Walking trails wind across the hillside and the best way to enjoy the zoo is to take the aerial safari ride to the top of the grounds and then zigzag back down through the zoo on the various walking trails to the ferry wharf at the bottom.

PREVIOUS PAGES, LEFT *An elephant's-eye view from Sydney's world-famous Taronga Zoo is just a short ferry ride from the high-rise metropolis across the harbour.*

PREVIOUS PAGES, RIGHT *The Tasmanian Devil lives in the wild in Tasmania only, so Taronga Zoo allows visitors a rare chance to meet up with this little renegade.*

A uniquely Australian encounter

The **Main Entrance** to the Taronga Zoo is a wonderful copper-domed building adorned with stucco animals dating from the zoo's earliest days. At the information booth you can pick up a map which also outlines the times for animal feedings, special presentations and zookeeper talks. Daily events include **Koala Encounters**, when visitors can be photographed with koalas, seal shows at the **Seal Theatre**, rainforest bird feeding, and talks by the keepers of chimpanzees, giraffes, dingoes, seals and reptiles.

Near the main entrance is the **Australian Walkabout**, home to kangaroos, wombats and other Australian native mammals. Adjacent is the very popular Koala Encounter where visitors can view these cute marsupials sitting in the crooks of trees munching on eucalyptus leaves, their only food. Nearby, where it can be viewed in its underwater habitat, is the bizarre platypus with its seal-like fur, beaver-like tail, webbed feet and bill like a duck's. The platypus is a monotreme, an egg-laying mammal which also suckles its young. Along with the platypus, the only other monotreme mammal in the world is the odd-looking spiny echidna which can also be viewed at the zoo.

OPPOSITE *One of the most popular animal houses at Taronga Zoo is the Asiatic Elephant enclosure. The population of Asiatic Elephants is in serious decline, so the zoo provides a safe haven.*

TOP *Reminiscent of the British-colonial presence in an exotic foreign country, the main entrance to Taronga Zoo is the gateway to the animal kingdom.*

RIGHT *The short-beaked echidnas share an exhibit with the platypus. Both are monotremes, egg-laying mammals that suckle their young.*

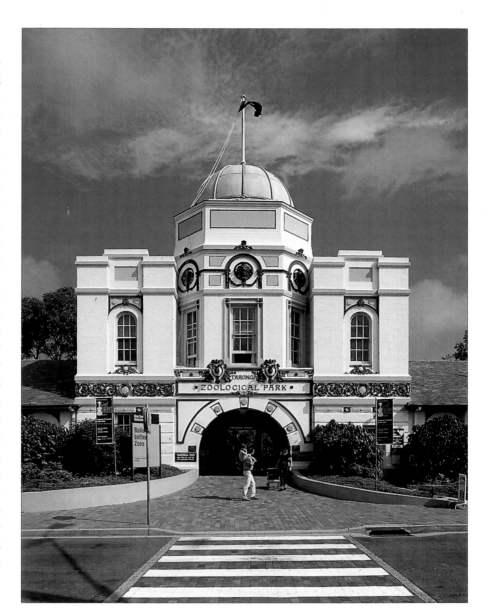

117

A Day at the Zoo

ABOVE *The aerial cabin ride is a great way to see the zoo's attractions as it hovers between the wharf and the front entrance.*

LEFT *The giraffes, residents of the African Waterhole exhibit, have one of the best views of the 'House'.*

OPPOSITE *Emus, along with other Australian birds, are located in the zoo's south-east corner.*

International residents

Across the hill on the other side of the entrance are the **Rainforest Birds** and also the **Orang-utan Rainforest** where the magnificent primates swing effortlessly through a simulated tropical forest environment. Nearby is **Serpentaria**, a new centre for conservation and research on reptiles, amphibians and invertebrates. Here you can see giant snakes like the anaconda and reticulated python, and the world's largest lizard, the frightening Komodo dragon, as well as a variety of frogs, snakes and lizards native to Australia. Head further west for the **Chimpanzee Park** where the agile primates never fail to entertain children and adults alike.

Wander down the hillside for the large African animals like giraffes, which enjoy one of the world's best views. At the

African Waterhole are hippopotamus and zebra, and further down are the fearsome Kodiak bears. In the centre of the park is the latest display, the African Tropical Forest.

North-east of here is the **Seal Theatre**, home to the playful seals and penguins, and then to the south are the elephants, the **Jungle Cats** – including such rare and seldom-seen creatures as the elusive snow leopard and the endangered Sumatran Tiger – and the **Australian Birds** in the south-east corner near the harbour shore.

From here you can head west to the ferry entrance and catch the bus or aerial safari ride back to the top, or walk to the nearby ferry wharf for the return ride to Circular Quay and the city.

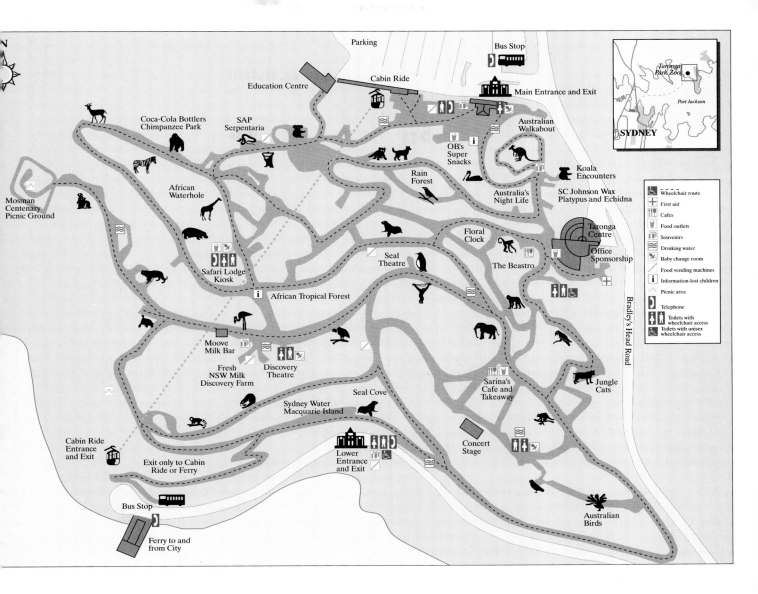

Parking

Bus Stop

Education Centre

Cabin Ride

Main Entrance and Exit

Coca-Cola Bottlers Chimpanzee Park

SAP Serpentaria

Australian Walkabout

OB's Super Snacks

Koala Encounters

African Waterhole

Rain Forest

Mosman Centenary Picnic Ground

Australia's Night Life

SC Johnson Wax Platypus and Echidna

Taronga Centre

Floral Clock

Office Sponsorship

Safari Lodge Kiosk

Seal Theatre

The Beastro

African Tropical Forest

Bradley's Head Road

Moove Milk Bar

Discovery Theatre

Fresh NSW Milk Discovery Farm

Sarina's Cafe and Takeaway

Jungle Cats

Seal Cove

Sydney Water Macquarie Island

Cabin Ride Entrance and Exit

Concert Stage

Exit only to Cabin Ride or Ferry

Lower Entrance and Exit

Bus Stop

Australian Birds

Ferry to and from City

SYDNEY · Taronga Park Zoo · Port Jackson

♿	Wheelchair route
✚	First aid
☕	Cafes
▯	Food outlets
≋	Drinking water
✂	Baby change room
╱	Food vending machines
i	Information-lost children
🧺	Picnic area
☎	Telephone
♿	Toilets with wheelchair access
♿	Toilets with unisex wheelchair access

Useful Information

Taronga Zoo is open daily from 9am to 5pm, and is also open at night for a limited season. Ferries to the zoo depart from Wharf 2 at **Circular Quay** every half-hour, commencing at 7.15am during the week, 8.45am on Saturdays and 9am on Sundays. The trip takes about 12 minutes. A bus connects from the zoo wharf and runs to the top gates, or visitors can take the **aerial safari ride** for a spectacular bird's-eye view of the zoo and the harbour. Purchase a ZooPass at Circular Quay which includes ferry, bus and aerial safari rides. An adult ticket costs $16 and $8.50 for children.

Tel: 1900 920218 (recorded message) or 9969–2777.

A Day at the Zoo

Harbourside Walks

Special Itinerary

HARBOURSIDE WALKS

Sydney's harbour foreshores provide an astonishing variety of walks, many of which have been covered in the various day tours around the city. These included the waterside walk from **The Rocks** to the **Royal Botanic Gardens** (*see* Day 1), **Darling Harbour** (*see* Day 3), the southern foreshores (*see* Day 4), **Manly** (*see* Day 5), and **Balmain** and other western harbour walks (*see* Day 6). The following three walks are on the northern foreshores and complement your exploration of Sydney Harbour.

Mosman Bay

This is a pleasant, easy 40-minute stroll, offering panoramic views as it winds around a delightful bay.

From **Circular Quay** take the ferry from wharf 4 to **Cremorne Point**. Climb the stairs and walk to the end of the promontory for fabulous views across to **Rose Bay** and of the **Harbour Bridge**. Walk back towards the wharf and take the right-hand path which leads around the shoreline of **Mosman Bay**.

Coastal bushland fringes the foreshores and small paths lead down to the rocks, while on the left-hand side of the path the exotic gardens of Mosman's exclusive residences spill down the hillside. Yachts bobbing at their moorings are the only evidence today of the bay's maritime history, which once included a whaling and shipbuilding centre during the 1830s.

PREVIOUS PAGES, LEFT *The Spit Bridge is surrounded by boat moorings. Beyond the bridge lies Fisher Bay and Clontarf Beach.*

PREVIOUS PAGES, RIGHT *The Spit Bridge raises its centre span at various times to allow ships to pass through into Middle Harbour.*

ABOVE *Cremorne Point divides Shell Cove and Mosman Bay; it harbourside homes are stylish with great views across to the city.*

OPPOSITE *Neutral Bay, Shell Cove and Mosman Bay provid peaceful inlets from the busy main waterway.*

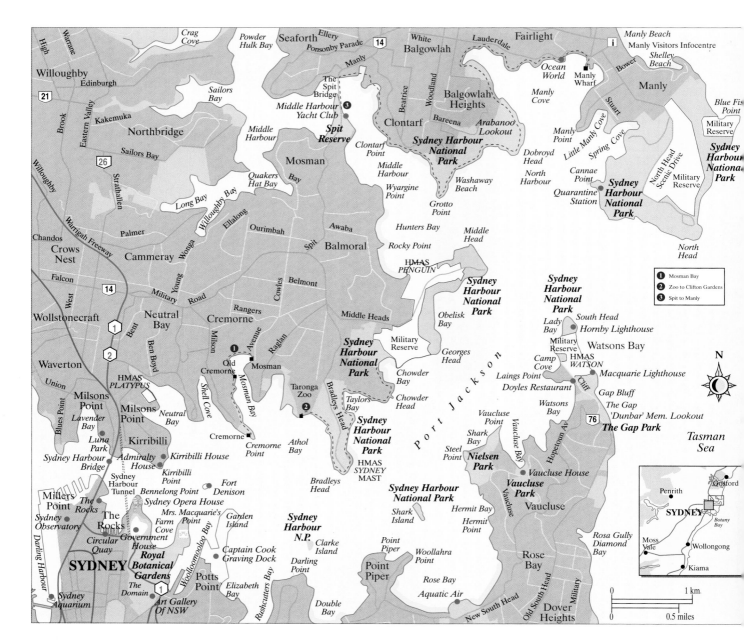

The walk passes magnificent gardens planted by Lex and Ruby Graham, (where a plaque commemorates their voluntary works), passes **Old Cremorne Wharf**, crosses a little bridge, and then winds around through **Harnett Park** where stairs lead down to the **Mosman Rowing Club**. Continue around the bay past **The Barn**, Mosman's oldest surviving building which was once a whaling storehouse, to **Mosman wharf** where you can catch the ferry back to Circular Quay.

The Zoo to Clifton Gardens

This 90-minute to 2-hour walk begins at **Taronga Zoo ferry wharf** and winds around the foreshores through part of **Sydney Harbour National Park** to **Clifton Gardens'** beach. From the wharf walk up **Athol Wharf Road** and follow the

path around the waterfront into the national park – a bird and animal sanctuary. Pass the picnic grounds of **Ashton Park** and walk out to **Bradleys Head** with its superb harbour panoramas. On the point is a lighthouse and the mast of the World War I naval cruiser HMAS *Sydney*.

Continue around the point, through bush and patches of rainforest for **Taylors Bay**. Look out for the last house beside the trail, **The Manor**, built at the turn of the century and walk up the stairs beside it to Morella Road. On the right is **Sarah's Walk**, which leads to Clifton Gardens bathing enclosure and parklands. You can go for a swim or picnic here before you catch the number 235 bus to Bradleys Head Road, where the walk down the hill leads back to the Taronga Zoo wharf.

The Spit to Manly

One of the world's most scenic harbour walking tracks is the 10-kilometre foreshore trail from **The Spit** to **Manly**. It was opened in 1988 as part of Australia's bicentennial celebrations. The trail takes around three–four hours to complete and passes through foreshore scenery, sculpted sandstone cliffs, heathlands, forests and beaches, which have changed little in 200 years of European occupation.

To begin the walk catch a number 182 (Narrabeen) or 184 (Mona Vale) bus from Wynyard in the city to The Spit. Walk across the **Spit Bridge** to the north, down the stairs on the left and then under the bridge. Follow the eastern trail along the old tramline, then through a pocket of rainforest to **Fisher Bay**, around the point to **Sandy Bay**, and on to **Clontarf**. These popular parklands hit world headlines in 1886 when Queen Victoria's son, the then Prince of Wales, survived an assassination attempt.

Continue around the coast for **Castle Rock** in the Sydney Harbour National Park and across the bushlands of **Grotto Point**, where pink gums, banksias and wildflowers flourish. From the heights of the trail along to **Crater Cove Lookout**, the harbour views extend out to **The Heads** and are magnificent. Squatter huts built in the 1920s still survive and their inhabitants enjoy some of Sydney's best views.

The trail then moves around **Dobroyd Head** and detours to **Reef Beach**, where nude bathing is common. Continue along to **Forty Baskets Beach**, rumoured to be the number of fish that were once caught here, with its swimming baths. Rock carvings of fish and shields can also be found at this spot. Follow the walkway along the coastline around North Harbour, passing **Fairlight** and **Delwood Beach** until you arrive at **Manly Cove** where you can catch the ferry back to Circular Quay.

BELOW The mast of the HMAS Sydney at the end of Bradleys Head is a favourite landmark for passengers on the famous Manly ferry. The walk from the zoo to the exclusive suburb of Clifton Gardens passes through Ashton Park where the point and the mast are accessible. Ashton Park and Bradleys Head form part of the Sydney Harbour National Park.

125

Bushwalking in the Royal National Park

Special Itinerary

BUSHWALKING IN THE ROYAL NATIONAL PARK

Sprawling over 15 000 hectares on the southern fringes of Sydney's suburbs, the world's first national park (it took the title 'national park' four years before the USA's Yellowstone) is bordered to the north by **Port Hacking**, to the west by the Princes Highway and the railway, and to the south and east by the Pacific Ocean. Soaring sandstone cliffs, idyllic beaches, heathlands covered in wildflowers, rainforested gullies, eucalyptus forests, river valleys and wetlands make up the varied and spectacular scenery of the **Royal National Park**. Over 150 kilometres of walking trails wind through the park providing access to the wide range of scenery. Details of the trail maps are available at the Visitor Centre in **Audley**.

Bundeena coast walk

Bundeena, where the ferry docks, is a picturesque coastal settlement on the south side of Port Hacking and is the start of the acclaimed **Coast Walk**, which winds along clifftops, heathlands and beaches for 26 kilometres to **Otford** in the south. It can take two days to do the entire trip, but daytrippers can opt for the shorter version to **Little Marley**, a four-hour-return walk. From Bundeena Wharf walk around the coast eastwards to **Jibbon Beach**, detour to **Jibbon Head** to see Aboriginal rock carvings of marine creatures, then follow the coastal trail past the **Waterrun**, a 16-metre waterfall which plunges into the ocean.

PREVIOUS PAGES, LEFT *The sun rises over beautiful Garie Beach within the Royal National Park, the first such park to be protected by the government. Garie Beach has always been a very popular haunt for both surfers and beach fishermen, as well as Sydney's many sunworshippers.*

PREVIOUS PAGES, RIGHT *The dry sclerophyll woodland is one of the large range of different habitats, including rainforest, sand dunes, heath and wetlands, that constitute Sydney's 15 000-hectare Royal National Park. Visitors can swim in the park's lagoon, spend a day on the small lake or visit the Aboriginal carvings of sea creatures.*

Wonderful ocean views extend from the clifftop trail, and from **Marley Headland** the coastal views are commanding. The seas surge dangerously in **Big Marley**, which is considered unsafe for swimming, while the lagoon behind the sand dunes is a shelter for wetland birds.

The rock ledges south of this beach offer excellent rock fishing, and at Little Marley the sheltered cove is a fabulous place to stop and swim. You can also relax on the grass beside the freshwater stream before returning to Bundeena.

Deer Pool and Little Marley

This 9-kilometre-return walk starts across the road from the Marley car park (5.6 kilometres from the turnoff from Sir Bertram Stevens Drive). Follow the trail across the windswept sandstone heathland, which is alive with wildflowers in winter and spring. Look out for the pink boronias, flannel flowers, and Christmas bells.

After 45 minutes you should reach **Marley Creek** and the **Deer Pool**, where deer introduced in the park's early days often drink. Water cascades down a sandstone slope into a freshwater pool, great for a refreshing dip before embarking on the walk to the coast which winds through forests of pink angophoras and other eucalypts to meet with the fire trail which leads to **Big Marley Beach**. From here follow Walk 1 (above) to **Little Marley Beach** and return the same way via Big Marley and the Deer Pool.

TOP *Bream, leatherjackets, flathead, and trevally are just some of the many species of fish caught at Garie Beach in the Royal National Park. Being a coastal city, fishing is one of Sydney's favourite sports.*

OPPOSITE *The ancient sandstone rock walls near Garie Beach have been eroded and stained by centuries of fresh water rising and falling over the cliff face.*

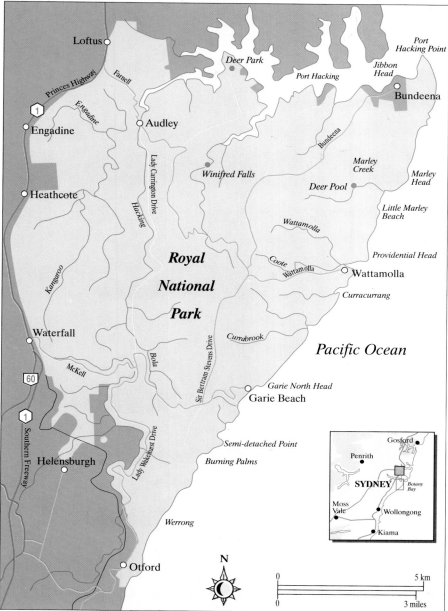

Bushwalking in the Royal National Park

Lady Carrington Drive

Head for the parklands at **Audley** beside the **Hacking River**. These are popular with picnickers and, for those who love the water, boats are available at the historic boatshed. The park's information centre, shop and kiosk are also located here. **Lady Carrington Drive**, originally built as a carriageway in 1886, is closed to cars but is perfect for cycling (bikes can be hired) and walking.

The trail follows the Hacking River to its rainforest source, passing creeks named after Aboriginal bird names, and there is a wide variety of birds and flora to be seen along the way. The 9.6-kilometre walk takes three hours one way so hikers can walk as long as they wish and then turn back. Choose from a number of idyllic picnic spots along the way and return along the same route to Audley and **Loftus**.

OPPOSITE TOP *An Australian native palm leans over the waters of Marley Creek which flows out of the spectacular Deer Pool.*

BELOW *The walls of the Deer Pool are reflected in the fresh water of Marley Creek which tempts those passing to cool off.*

ABOVE *A seagull keeps a watchful eye for any food that might appear in the shallows of the golden sands of Garie Beach.*

Useful Information

Visitors can reach the **Royal National Park** by car, train or ferry.

Car: Drive south from the city on the Princes Highway. Follow the signs and turn off for the park 2.5 kilometres south of Sutherland. There is a $7.50 fee to enter the national park with a car.

Train: A train runs every half-hour from **Central Railway Station** to **Loftus** on the South Coast line. On Sundays and public holidays a tourist tram meets the train and takes passengers into the national park; at other times follow the walking trail. To connect to the ferry catch the train from **Central** to **Cronulla**. Trains leave approximately every half-hour and take about 48 minutes.

Ferry: Ferries run every half-hour from **Gunnamatta Bay** to **Bundeena**. The ferry wharf is near the Tonkin Street exit of the Cronulla railway station.

Visitor Centre: Audley; open daily 9am–4pm; tel: 9542–0648.

Cruising Sydney's Waterways

Special Itinerary

CRUISING SYDNEY'S WATERWAYS

When the American novelist Mark Twain visited Sydney a century ago, his list of 'things to do' included a 'tour of the harbour in a fine steam pleasure launch'. These days a trip on Sydney's waterways is even more popular and the options of exploring them extend to ferries, express catamarans, cruisers, yachts, houseboats, water taxis, water limousines and historic sailing ships. There are over 50 different harbour cruises that depart daily from both **Circular Quay** and **Darling Harbour**, and the **Quayside Booking Centre** provides tickets and information at both points. Destinations are equally diverse and include: around the harbour's lengthy shoreline, **Middle Harbour**, **Lane Cove River**, **Parramatta River**, the waters of the flooded **Hawkesbury River Valley**, and **Pittwater**.

Scheduled cruises

Ferries are the cheapest, easiest and most traditional way to explore the harbour and many of the day tours around Sydney include ferry trips in their itineraries. Circular Quay is the hub of both state-run and private services to all sections of the harbour.

The state-run **Sydney Ferries** run large and small boats and express catamarans to over 30 different locations including **Manly** from wharves 2 & 3, **Taronga Zoo** from wharf 2, the eastern suburbs and northern shore from wharf 4, and western services to **Darling Harbour**, **Balmain** and up the **Parramatta River** from wharf 5. Sydney Ferries also operate a **Morning Harbour Cruise** of the main harbour from **Rose Bay** up the Parramatta River.

PREVIOUS PAGES, LEFT *Sydney's famous 'Southerly Bluster' blows in over the spit at Middle Harbour. Sydney's hot summer days can sometimes reach temperatures as high as 40°C and relief arrives in the shape of semi-tropical storms.*

PREVIOUS PAGES, RIGHT *An evening cruise is definitely the best way to see the city light up at night, especially Darling Harbour where there are a number of entertainment venues and several cafes and restaurants.*

OPPOSITE *The* Sydney Harbour Explorer *stops outside the Opera House before it continues its cruise around the harbour.*

ABOVE *The Spit Bridge links the northern beach suburbs to the harbourside suburbs of Balmoral and Mosman.*

BELOW *Middle Harbour is a great place for sailing, its popularity exemplified by the congestion of marinas lining its shores and bays.*

The **Afternoon Harbour Cruise** heads downstream to **Sydney Heads**, then diverts around the picturesque waterways of Middle Harbour. The 90-minute **Evening Harbour Lights Cruise** provides a wonderful view of Sydney at night reflected in the harbour waters.

Many private cruise companies operate tours around the harbour's best-known sights. **Captain Cook Cruises** run a **Sydney Harbour Explorer** which departs four times a day from wharf 6 and stops off at the Opera House, Watsons Bay, Taronga Zoo, Darling Harbour and The Rocks. Passengers can alight and reboard the later cruises. **Matilda and Sail Venture Cruises** also operate a number of daily harbour tours, including their sailing catamarans. **Bounty Cruises** include daily brunch, lunch and dinner cruises on the *Bounty*, a replica of Captain Bligh's 18th-century vessel built for the movie *Mutiny on the Bounty* starring Mel Gibson. It departs from Campbells Cove in The Rocks. **Sydney By Sail**, a 90-minute harbour tour organised by the National Maritime Museum, introduces visitors to the art of sailing while viewing Sydney's sights.

Cruising Sydney's Waterways

Sailing on your own

A number of firms offer boat charter facilities. **Flagship Charters** hire out their private fleet of yachts, luxury motor cruises and even a 1933 replica wooden speedboat for private charter. You can sail yourself or charter skippered yachts from **Ausail Yacht Charters**. **Church Point Charter** allows you to explore beautiful Pittwater (*see* Day 5) aboard self-drive cruisers, yachts or catamarans.

Perhaps the fastest and most personalised way to get around Sydney Harbour is by hailing one of the **Harbour Taxi Boats**. They offer services to all the sights and to famous waterside restaurants and the **Fish Markets**.

Hawkesbury River options

Brooklyn, a waterside hamlet on the Hawkesbury River accessible by both **CityRail** (Gosford line) and road (Sydney–Newcastle Freeway), is the centre for hiring houseboats and cruisers to explore the scenic waterways of the **Ku-ring-gai Chase National Park**. For a fascinating look at life in the tiny riverside settlements of the Hawkesbury, **Australia's Last Riverboat Postman Cruise** follows the mail run upriver. This popular four-hour cruise includes morning tea. **Hawkesbury River Ferries** run this cruise as well as a scenic trip around the national park viewing Aboriginal rock carvings and historical sights, and they stop off at the famous **Berowra Waters Settlement** for lunch. Bookings for Hawkesbury River cruises can be made at the Quayside Booking Centre (*see* above) or the NSW State Railways. **Holidays-A-Float** hire two-berth to 10-berth houseboats and cruisers, as do **Ripples Houseboat Hire**.

OPPOSITE *Just off the northern freeway and only a little over 20 kilometres north of Pearces Corner is Brooklyn, located on the banks of the Hawkesbury River. Squeezed between the river and the cliffs that rise up behind the village, Brooklyn has a collection of interesting building styles that give the place a character of its own. Slowly being gentrified, it is an exclusive suburb of Sydney and the Central Coast.*

BELOW *At the headwaters of Cowan Creek lies Bobbin Head, an idyllic watershed in the Ku-ring-gai Chase National Park. Nestled into the upper North Shore and encircled by Duffy's Forest, St Ives, North Wahroonga, Mount Colah and Mount Ku-ring-gai, Bobbin Head is the park's most developed area and is very close to large population centres, providing a perfect retreat for fishing, cruising and other recreational pursuits.*

Useful Information

Ausail Yacht Charters: The Spit; tel: 9960–5511.

Australia's Last Riverboat Postman Cruise: departs Brooklyn daily 9.30am; adults $30, children $15; *see* Hawkesbury River Ferries.

Captain Cook Cruises: No. 6 Jetty, Circular Quay; departs daily from 9.30am; adults $18, children $13; tel: 9206–1111.

Church Point Charter: 122 Crescent Road, Newport; tel: 9999–4188.

Flagship Charters: tel: 9555–5901.

Harbour Taxi Boats: tel: 9555–1155.

Hawkesbury River Ferries, tel: 9985–7566.

Holidays-A-Float: tel: 9985–7368.

Matilda and Sail Venture Cruises: Pier 26, Darling Harbour; departs daily from 9.30am; adults $24, children $12; tel: 9264–7377.

Quayside Booking Centre: tel: 9247–5151.

Ripples Houseboat Hire: tel: 9985–7333.

Sydney By Sail: tel: 9552–7561.

Sydney Bus, Train and Ferries info line: 13 1500. Morning Harbour Cruise departs daily 11.15am from wharf 4, returns 12.30pm; adults $13, children $8.50.

Afternoon Harbour Cruise departs daily 1pm, returns 3.30pm; adults $19, children $12.

Evening Harbour Lights Cruise departs 8pm; $16.50 adults, $10.50 children.

Bounty Cruises: tel: 9247–1789.

Vagabond Cruises: East Circular Quay; departs daily from 11.00am; adults from $20, children from $10; tel: 9660–0388.

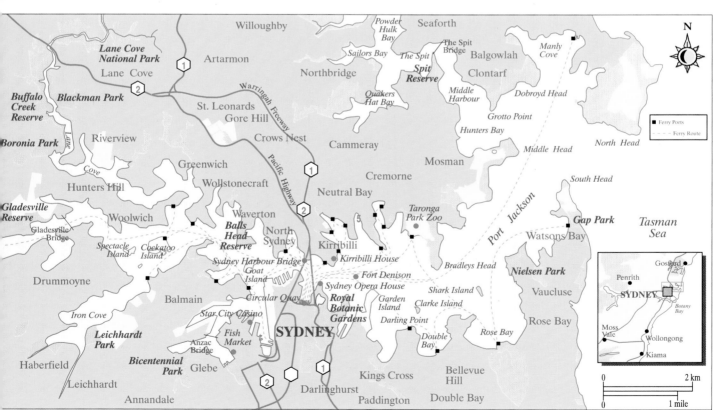

Willoughby

Lane Cove
National Park
Lane Cove
Artarmon

Powder
Hulk
Bay
Seaforth

Sailors Bay
The Spit
Bridge
Balgowlah

Manly
Cove

The Spit
Spit
Reserve
Clontarf

N

Buffalo
Creek
Reserve
Blackman Park

Northbridge

St. Leonards
Gore Hill

Warringah Freeway

Quakers
Hat Bay

Middle
Harbour

Dobroyd Head

Grotto Point

North Head

Ferry Ports
Ferry Route

Boronia Park

Riverview

Crows Nest

Cammeray

Hunters Bay

Middle Head

Hunters Hill

Greenwich

Pacific Highway

Wollstonecraft

Cremorne

Mosman

South Head

Gladesville
Reserve

Woolwich

Gladesville
Bridge

Lane Cove

Neutral Bay

Waverton
Balls
Head
Reserve
North
Sydney

Kirribilli

Taronga
Park Zoo

Port Jackson

Gap Park

Watsons Bay

Tasman
Sea

Gosford

Spectacle
Island
Cockatoo
Island

Sydney Harbour Bridge

Kirribilli House

Bradleys Head

Nielsen Park

Penrith

SYDNEY

Drummoyne

Goat Island
Circular Quay

Fort Denison

Sydney Opera House
Royal
Botanic
Gardens

Shark Island

Vaucluse

Botany
Bay

Iron Cove

Balmain

Star City Casino

Garden
Island
Clarke Island

Rose Bay

Moss
Vale

Wollongong

Leichhardt
Park

Fish
Market

Anzac
Bridge

Darling Point

Double
Bay

Rose Bay

Kiama

Haberfield

Bicentennial
Park

Glebe

SYDNEY

Double
Bay

0   2 km

Leichhardt

Annandale

Darlinghurst
Paddington

Kings Cross

Bellevue
Hill

Double Bay

0   1 mile

Cruising Sydney's Waterways

Central Coast Getaway

Special Itinerary

CENTRAL COAST GETAWAY

The **Central Coast** is located north of Sydney and is renowned for its waterways, beaches and leisurely lifestyle. It is a favourite weekend getaway for many Sydneysiders. The best way to explore the region is by car, but it is also accessible by rail and bus, and a number of companies offer daytrip tours from Sydney.

A great round trip by car is to leave Sydney via the Harbour Bridge and follow the **Pacific Highway** signs to Newcastle. Enter the **Sydney–Newcastle (F3) Freeway**, which grants spectacular scenery as it crosses the Hawkesbury River, straddles high ridges, and cuts through sandstone hills offering panoramic views of **Ku-ring-gai Chase National Park** and its fjord-like river valleys. Take the Gosford exit and follow the signs for Old Sydney Town.

Old Sydney Town – a living museum

Old Sydney Town is NSW's largest heritage-theme park. It is an authentic recreation of Sydney as it was in 1788 with actors living out the life of the early days of the colony. There are popular whippings of convicts which are well staged while the buildings are faithfully recreated and include a gaol, a church, a windmill, cottages with thatched or shingled roofs and Lieutenant Dawe's Observatory. From here continue on to Gosford.

Scenic drive

Gosford, the commercial centre of the Central Coast, is placed at the head of picturesque **Brisbane Water**. This area is very popular with boating enthusiasts. From the **Entrance Road** to the east turn right onto **Avoca Drive** to **Kincumber**.

PREVIOUS PAGES, LEFT *The Skillion is a headland which rises above a dramatic rock shelf at the Central Coast town of Terrigal, a popular honeymoon and weekend getaway for Sydneysiders.*

PREVIOUS PAGES, RIGHT *A team of powerful Clydesdales takes a group of visitors around the streets of Old Sydney Town. This theme park allows visitors to slide back in time to the 18th century.*

OPPOSITE *The warm sands of Terrigal Beach are overlooked by the Skillion. Surprisingly, the climate at the Central Coast is significantly warmer than Sydney, which is why the area attracts large numbers of visitors and provides an alternative to city living.*

RIGHT *A small flotilla of inboard motor boats, or 'putt putts' as they are affectionately called, lie at their moorings on the calm waters of The Entrance, a popular resort town at the head of Tuggerah Lake.*

BOTTOM *Actors dressed in period costume portray the brutal method of punishment employed in the early days of the colony. Scenes like these are typical of what visitors can participate in and observe at Old Sydney Town.*

A pleasant detour is **The Scenic Drive** which winds through the **Bouddi National Park** with its majestic cliffs and ocean views, and then continues over the **Rip Bridge** to the excellent surfing area of **Ocean Beach**. Beyond here is **Pearl Beach** which has chic cafes and wonderful hideaways if you want to spend the night. Further down Avoca Drive is **Avoca Beach**, a quiet weekend retreat.

The **Scenic Highway** continues on to picturesque **Terrigal** where cafes and restaurants offer a variety of lunches. Try the **Haven Beach Cafe** housed in the old fish co-op where outdoor dining on the balcony provides sweeping vistas of the beach (*see* Cuisine). From Terrigal follow the coast road, where smaller roads branch off to picturesque beaches like **Toowoon Bay**, home of the luxury **Kim's Beachside Retreat**, and head north to **The Entrance**. This old-style holiday mecca at the head of **Tuggerah Lake** is renowned for its fishing and its prolific pelicans, which are fed daily at 3.30pm in the **Memorial Park** at The Entrance.

Macquarie – an impressive coastal lake

If you continue up the coast road you'll pass the fishing resort of **Budgewoi** to rejoin the Pacific Highway at **Doyalson**. North of here is **Lake Macquarie**, Australia's largest coastal lake with over 170 kilometres of foreshore and more than 34 launching ramps for boats. It is a great place for sailing, boating and fishing. At **Swansea**, where the lake enters the sea, fishermen pull in huge flatheads, and there are lakeside parklands at **Belmont**, **Warners Bay** and **Toronto** around the northern foreshore.

Central Coast Getaway

Newcastle – the city of coal

Follow the highway north to **Newcastle**, NSW's second largest city, which is fast out-growing its 'Coal City' industrial image. Newcastle offers visitors excellent city beaches, fine historical buildings and a revamped waterfront with cafes and parklands. Wedged between the ocean and the **Hunter River**, Newcastle's commercial centre contains superb 19th-century buildings including the Gothic-style **Newcastle Cathedral**. The newly-restored **Queens Wharf** area is along the city's waterfront, and Beaumont Street in nearby **Hamilton** has a variety of restaurants and cafes offering cosmopolitan dining.

The rocky promontory at the southern harbour entrance, known as **Nobbys**, was once an island, while nearby **Fort Scratchley** which now houses the interesting **Maritime Museum**, was built as a fortification against the possibility of a Russian invasion in the 1870s. It is also the only fort on the Australian mainland to have fired its guns in defence against an enemy. The incident occurred when a Japanese submarine entered the harbour in 1942.

From here you can return to Sydney by following the signs to the Freeway and heading south.

BELOW *The Tasman Sea breaks onto the beaches of Bouddi National Park. While the Central Coast is attracting more residents, there are still many places that provide a respite from the material world.*

OPPOSITE TOP *Newcastle is bordered by the Pacific Ocean and the Hunter River.*

OPPOSITE CENTRE *The main street of Gosford is a busy shopping area.*

OPPOSITE BOTTOM *Avoca Beach, often chosen for surfing competitions, is a great place to swim, walk, surf or bodyboard. Several different sandbanks create a selection of breaks from which to choose.*

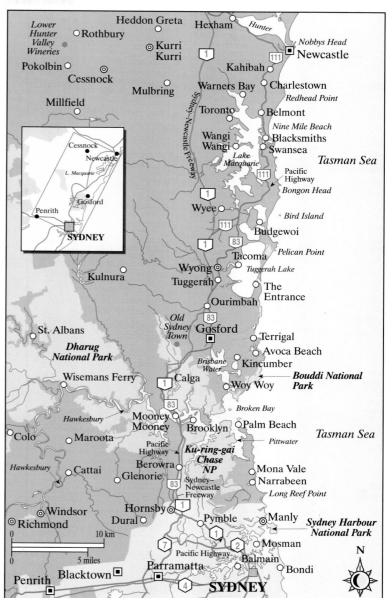

Lower Hunter Valley Wineries
Rothbury
Heddon Greta
Hexham
Hunter
Nobbys Head
Newcastle
Kurri Kurri
Kahibah
Pokolbin
Cessnock
Warners Bay
Charlestown
Mulbring
Redhead Point
Millfield
Toronto
Belmont
Nine Mile Beach
Wangi Wangi
Blacksmiths
Lake Macquarie
Swansea
Tasman Sea
Pacific Highway
Bongon Head
Wyee
Bird Island
Budgewoi
Pelican Point
Tacoma
Kulnura
Wyong
Tuggerah Lake
Tuggerah
The Entrance
Ourimbah
Old Sydney Town
Gosford
Terrigal
Avoca Beach
St. Albans
Kincumber
Dharug National Park
Brisbane Water
Bouddi National Park
Wisemans Ferry
Calga
Woy Woy
Broken Bay
Hawkesbury
Mooney Mooney
Brooklyn
Palm Beach
Colo
Maroota
Pacific Highway
Pittwater
Tasman Sea
Hawkesbury
Cattai
Berowra
Glenorie
Ku-ring-gai Chase NP
Mona Vale
Narrabeen
Long Reef Point
Windsor
Richmond
Hornsby
Dural
Pymble
Manly
Sydney Harbour National Park
Mosman
Pacific Highway
Balmain
Penrith
Blacktown
Parramatta
Bondi
SYDNEY

Cessnock
Newcastle
L. Macquarie
Gosford
Penrith
SYDNEY

10 km
5 miles

N

Winelover's Tour of the Hunter Valley

Special Itinerary

The **Hunter Valley** is Australia's oldest commercial wine-producing region and is renowned internationally for its rich, full-bodied wines. A wine-tasting tour around the vineyards (the region boasts over 50) makes for a great daytrip. Various tour companies conduct excursions to the region, and **Hunter Valley Tourism Services** can organise wine and cheese tasting tours. As the Hunter is only a two-hour drive north of Sydney, nothing beats having your own car to explore the valley freely.

From Sydney take the **Newcastle Freeway** (*see* Central Coast) and exit before Newcastle for Cessnock. **Cessnock** is an historic coal-mining town now famous as the gateway to the vineyards and wineries of the Hunter Valley. At Cessnock follow the signs to the tourist information centre on the corner of Wollombi and Mount View roads to pick up maps and information.

Pleasant tastings

The roads seem to loop around the region creating a circular drive, which takes in the major wineries. Head up **Mount View Road** to the end, turn right into **Oakey Creek Road** and then left into **Marrowbone Road** for the McWilliam family's 75-year-old **Mount Pleasant Winery**. They conduct guided tours and offer wine-tasting, including Australia's most awarded white wine, Elizabeth Semillon.

PREVIOUS PAGES, LEFT *As soon as the sun begins to set behind the hills, the temperature drops, the mist rolls in and dew drops start to form on the grapes that hang invitingly on the vines. The verdant slopes of the Hunter Valley are recognised as Australia's oldest commercial wine-producing region.*

PREVIOUS PAGES, RIGHT *Tyrrells is one of Australia's best known and most distinguished wine producers. Their large oak barrels store the wine till it is aged, which gives it a unique flavour and bouquet. Situated off Broke Road, Tyrrells is just a stone's throw from the Pokolbin Flora Reserve.*

Continue north through the **Pokolbin Valley** on McDonalds Road to **Lindeman's Hunter River** winery. They have a fascinating **Winemaking Museum**. Further along is the **Pokolbin Estate Vineyard**. At the junction of McDonalds and Broke roads turn right for **Blaxland's Restaurant**. If you then turn right into Halls Road you'll come to **Pepper Tree Wines**, which is set in romantic gardens with an old barn that services as an excellent wine-tasting venue.

Back on Broke Road, head back to the junction to **Hungerford Hill Wine Village**, a popular tourist stopover with picnic grounds, children's playground, gift shop, restaurant, and of course cellar-door wine-tasting. Further along Broke Road is **Tyrrells**, where award-winning wines have been produced for over a century.

OPPOSITE *Lindeman's wines are an institution in Australia's wine industry. At their winery you can taste the product and also find out how wine has been made over the last century at their museum.*

BELOW *Barrels and bottles combine to create the ideal ambience for the wine buff. Cellars are a great place to sample the fruit of the vine.*

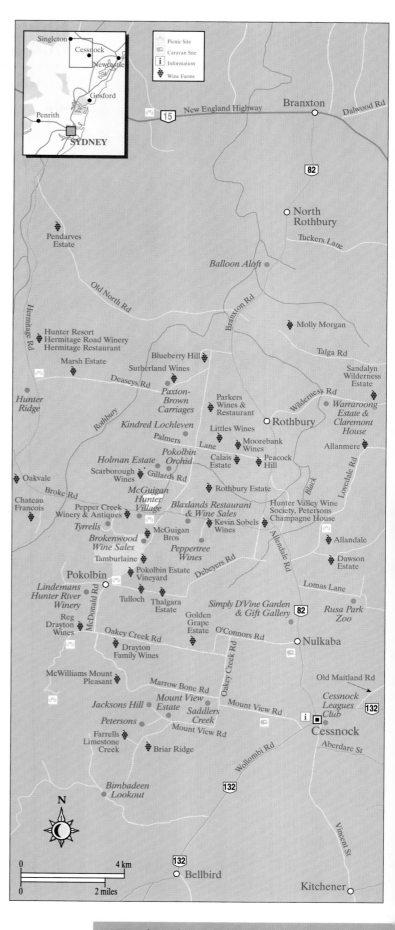

Winelover's Tour of the Hunter Valley

Useful Information

Cessnock Visitor Centre: tel: 4990–4477.

Hunter Valley Day Tours: tel: 4938–5031.

WINERIES

Mount Pleasant Winery: open daily 10am–4.30pm;
tours 11am; tel: 4998-7505.

Lindeman's Cellar Door: tel: 4998-7684.

Pokolbin Estate Vineyard: daily 10am–6pm; tel: 4998–7524.

Pepper Tree Wines: tel: 4998-7539.

McGuigan Cellars: tel: 4998-7402.

Tyrrell's: tel: 4993–7000.

Wyndham Estate: tel: 4938–3444.

RESTAURANTS

Chez Pok: Ekerts Road, tel: 4998-7596.

Olives Country House: Campbell's Lane, tel: 4998-7838.

Roberts at Pepper Tree: Halls Road, tel: 4998-7330.

SOMETHING DIFFERENT

Balloons Aloft; tel: 1800 028568.

Hunter Valley Motorcycle Tours; tel: 4938-7129.

Pokolbin Horse Coaches; tel: 4998-7305.

ABOVE *The Hunter Valley has been producing wines for many decades and is an internationally successful venture, thanks to the valley's perfect conditions.*

OPPOSITE TOP *The verandah of Peppers Guest House in the Pokolbin district is a superb place to relax, especially when the sunlight filters through the hanging baskets.*

OPPOSITE BOTTOM *Peppers Guest House is built in the colonial architecture style and has beautiful cottage gardens, making it a special place to spend the night.*

Turn right and head north along Hermitage Road for the **Hunter Estate** and the adjacent **Hunter Resort** surrounded by some of the 7 million vines which flourish in the valley. From here, visitors can opt to return to Pokolbin Valley or drive north to the New England Highway; turn right for **Branxton**, and continue to **Dalwood** for the **Wyndham Estate** beside the Hunter River, which offers more wine-tasting, pleasant picnic grounds and horse-drawn coach rides.

Back on the New England Highway head for Branxton and take Branxton Road south.

For something different

At **North Rothbury**, **Balloons Aloft** run sunrise hot-air balloon rides over the vineyards with a champagne breakfast to celebrate afterwards. Other interesting options around the Hunter include touring the region on the back of a **Harley-Davidson motorcycle** or taking a leisurely tour with **Pokolbin Horse Coaches** visiting wineries in old-style comfort.

For visitors wanting to stay overnight at Pokolbin in the heart of the vineyards there are a number of excellent guest-houses including colonial-style **Peppers**, The **Olives Country House** famed for its breakfasts, the award-winning **Hunter Resort**, or for a real treat spend a night at **The Convent Guest House**, which was once a turn-of-the-century nunnery.

Good food and wine are a perfect combination and the restaurants of the Hunter Valley are legendary, especially **Robert's at Peppertree**, **Chez Pok** at Peppers Guest House, and **Blaxland's** (*see* Cuisine).

The Southern Highlands

Special Itinerary

THE SOUTHERN HIGHLANDS

From early colonial days the elevated region known as the **Southern Highlands**, atop the Illawarra escarpment (around 120 kilometres south of the Sydney), was envisaged as a cool escape for the gentry. These days the label still fits; exclusive country homes nestle amongst rolling hills and on weekends the main street of **Bowral**, the unofficial capital, is lined with luxury cars. History, horses and horticulture are the biggest drawcards and because the Southern Highlands is only a 90-minute drive from the city it is a popular daytrip. This day tour can be easily combined with 'The South Coast' (*see* following pages) completing a circular route by road.

Blazing spring gardens

Head south from the city following the signs for Liverpool on the **Hume Highway**, then take the **South Western Freeway** (M5) and exit for the first highlands town of **Mittagong**, which boasts beautiful **Kennerton Green**, Australia's finest private garden. To get there turn left into Ferguson Crescent just before Mittagong, then right into Bong Bong Road and the gardens are located two kilometres on the right. They are open only in spring (September 21 to November 24) and the sweeping lawns and woodlands, ablaze with bluebells and freesias, are a 'must see' for garden lovers.

PREVIOUS PAGES, LEFT *The lush green fields, winding roads and pine tree windbreaks of the Clairsdale Stud Farm at Bowral reveal the rustic charm of the landscape of the Southern Highlands.*

PREVIOUS PAGES, RIGHT *The clock tower at the crossroads in the town of Mittagong in the Southern Highlands has seen billions of cars whizz past as they head south to either Melbourne or the coast.*

ABOVE *At the base of the Southern Highlands lies Kangaroo Valley, a fertile stretch of land where cattle love to range. It is the perennial rye grass encircled by hills that makes the valley so picturesque.*

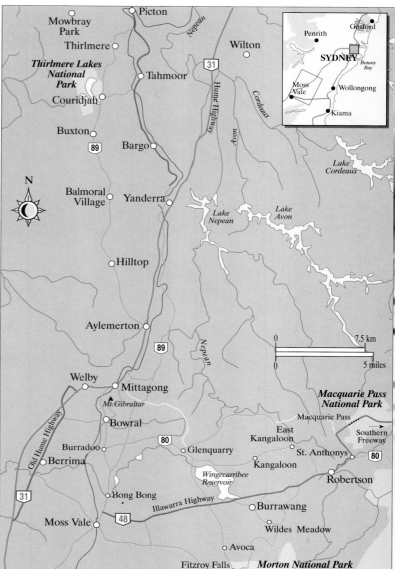

Back on the freeway, continue on for Bowral, venue of the annual **Tulip Festival** held in September/October. Bowral is a chic hub of fashionable cafes, antique shops, boutiques specialising in country-style apparel, and elegant old-world-style hotels and guesthouses. The **Bradman Museum** in Glebe Park honours Bowral's most famous resident, the cricketing great, Sir Donald Bradman, and is open daily from 10am to 4pm. Bowral also boasts a number of private gardens which are open throughout the year, like **Buskers End** on St Clair Street with its majestic trees and cool-climate shrubs; also including the National Collection of hydrangeas. For garden-opening times contact the **Southern Highlands Visitor Information Centre**.

Berrima – National Trust town

Cross the railway line and head west towards **Berrima**, the region's most historic town which has stayed in a time-warp ever since the rail bypassed it in the 1860s. This entire colonial township from the Georgian-era is now listed by the National Trust and its major heritage buildings include the still-operable **Gaol**, the **Courthouse**, and the **Surveyor General Inn**, one of Australia's oldest, continually licensed hotels. Berrima is oriented towards visitors and gift shops encourage browsing while the cafes and tearooms beckon hungry travellers.

Valleys of green

From Berrima head south on the **Old Hume Highway** and turn east for **Moss Vale** where travellers can board an exciting steam train for the **South Coast**, shop for antiques, or continue exploring the highlands by taking the **Nowra Road** to the magnificent **Fitzroy Falls**. These waters plunge dramatically 80 metres to the floor of

ABOVE *The town of Bowral holds an annual Tulip Festival in spring.*

TOP *Doughty deeds with willow clubs and leather spheres are a knockout on the field at the Bradman Cricket Museum in Bowral.*

The Southern Highlands

ABOVE *The blackboard menu outside a Berrima cafe displays the English influence that many of the town's historic buildings retain.*

TOP *On the road to Robertson lies Milton Park Hotel, the ideal country retreat for those who want to escape to luxury and style.*

LEFT *The Fitzroy Falls plunge 80 metres from the top of Illawarra escarpment onto the rocks below.*

OPPOSITE *White fences and small rectangular paddocks are the tell-tale signs of a horse stud, a thriving industry of the Southern Highlands.*

the rugged Morton National Park. Guided tours of the walking trails are offered from the **Visitor Centre**, which also has a cafe.

From the falls, motorists can continue along the winding road down the escarpment to **Kangaroo Valley** (*see* South Coast), or continue to explore the Highlands by following Shellwash Road north, past **Avoca**, and then right for **Wildes Meadow** and left for **Burrawang**, a timeless hamlet where an historic **General Store** has been continuously trading for 130 years. Drop into the **Dining Room Antiques** in the old schoolhouse for coffee and a browse around the antique porcelains and homewares.

From **Burrawang**, head east along the Illawarra Highway for **Robertson**, heart of 'potato country' and more recently famed as the location for *Babe*, the award-winning Australian movie about a talking pig. The pottery and handicraft shops are a good place to browse. Then continue down the Illawarra Highway and through the spectacular **Macquarie Pass**.

The road at this point links up to the Southern Freeway back to Sydney or, alternatively, you could take the delightful rural road north and then west through **Kangaloon** and back to Bowral. Just after the Bong Bong racetrack, about 6 kilometres from Bowral's centre, look out for **Milton Park** on the left on Horderns Road. This stately residence, once the home of department-store tycoons, is now a luxury hotel surrounded by 285 hectares of grounds where guests can horse ride or enjoy a leisurely game of croquet. For those who can afford it, Milton Park provides an authentic highlands' country-house experience with excellent contemporary cuisine (*see* Cuisine) and is a perfect finale for a tour of the region.

The South Coast

Special Itinerary

THE SOUTH COAST

Timeless, unhurried, tucked between the mountains and the sea with undoubtedly the most spectacular scenery within a day's drive of Sydney, the **South Coast** has always been a favourite retreat for writers and artists, beach-goers and fishermen, and for visitors seeking a tranquil escape from the city. The celebrated English novelist D.H. Lawrence stayed in the region in 1922 and wrote his famous novel, *Kangaroo*. The journey south and the detours along the way are easiest to explore by car.

Winding wilderness

Begin by taking the **Princes Highway** out of Sydney, and then turn onto the Southern Freeway. Exit onto the Old Princes Highway for **Stanwell Park**. Another alternative scenic but longer route is via the **Royal National Park** which, like Old Princes Highway, exits the bush and merges on the coast road at Stanwell Tops. The Tops are well known for the rainbow-coloured hang-gliders who soar above Bald Hill and for the panorama of scalloped beaches and cliffs that plunge into the vast blue Pacific Ocean – a breathtaking sight indeed. The road winds through lush rainforest to the tranquil beach hamlet of Stanwell Park, which was once the home of a famous Australian aviation pioneer, Lawrence Hargrave, who is also remembered on Bald Hill by a memorial plaque.

PREVIOUS PAGES, LEFT *Part of Wollongong's fishing fleet moors in the protected waters of Wollongong Harbour. Wollongong, the capital of the South Coast, is the home of steel-producing industries, a large ethnic population, fabulous surfing beaches and the Steelers Rugby League Club.*

PREVIOUS PAGES, RIGHT *Friesian cows graze peacefully on green paddocks of lucerne and clover near the village of Berry.*

ABOVE *A war memorial in a central park in the small South Coast village of Kiama.*

For the next 15 kilometres south, the road winds around near-vertical cliffs with the surging Pacific Ocean below – one of Australia's most spectacular drives. It passes tiny coal-mining towns, and connects to the town of Thirroul where Wyewurk, D.H. Lawrence's Australian residence, stands at No. 3 Craig Street. The house is not open to the public but it is still (after a lengthy battle by conservationists against proposed extensions) in its original condition. Visitors can wander along the beach to glimpse Lawrence's old retreat, which is described along with Thirroul in his novel.

Wollongong – beaches and steel

Continue south for **Wollongong**, 'The Steel City', where industrial complexes contrast with the natural charms of this coastal city. Wollongong boasts wonderful beaches, a botanic garden, a university and the largest Buddhist temple in the Southern Hemisphere, which is hard to miss.

The enormous orange-coloured **Nan Tien Temple** has red-tiled roofs and matching pagodas in a massive complex which sprawls over an area exceeding 22 hectares. Continue along the coastal drive, past the fishing boats in **Wollongong Harbour** and the **City Beach** to **Port Kembla's** dynamic industrial area, where its harbour bustles with cargo ships. At the port, **Australia's Industry World** runs tours, giving an inside glimpse to the prime industry of the area.

Follow the coast road past expansive Lake Illawarra to **Shellharbour**, a popular surfing and fishing spot which is rapidly becoming another Wollongong suburb. Rejoin the Princes Highway and continue south to **Kiama**, a scenic coastal town, renowned for its **Blowhole**. The Blowhole is a natural rock formation which can produce geyser-like sprays over 50 metres high. This is an excellent spot to have a picnic by the sea or perhaps you should grab a snack in the **Terrace** tearooms which were once miners' cottages.

ABOVE *Kiama's famous Blowhole operates only when there is a big swell surging from the ocean. When it does blow it presents a spectacular performance.*

LEFT *Furnace stacks at Port Kembla are an unmistakable symbol of industry.*

BELOW *The entrance to Nan Tien Buddhist Temple, the largest in the Southern Hemisphere, is one of the most unexpected sights in Wollongong.*

ABOVE *Stanwell Tops offers a superb view of Wollongong's northern beach suburbs.*

BELOW *Bakeries, shops, pubs, cafes and restaurants line the main street of Berry.*

OPPOSITE *Nestled within a cove is the small town of Stanwell Park.*

Rolling green pastures

Head west 12 kilometres via **Jamberoo**, a peaceful dairy-farming valley and historic township, to **Minnamurra Rainforest**, part of the **Budderoo National Park**, where an elevated walkway leads under the soaring tree canopy to the falls. Return to the Princes Highway and follow the magnificent coastal drive south, looping around the rolling green hills that run right to the ocean's edge. Cross the railway line at **Gerringong** and leave the Princes Highway for the coastal route via **Gerroa**, where the panorama takes in expansive ocean views and the beautiful **Seven Mile Beach** to the south, fringed by the national park of the same name.

Turn inland to **Berry**, an historic town on the Princes Highway renowned for its heritage buildings, which house cafes, restaurants, and gift shops. The town has a number of eateries and is the nearest town to **Kangaroo Valley**, a fashionable rural retreat surrounded by mountains, only 17 kilometres to the west. Kangaroo Valley is famed for its 19th-century ambience and the sandstone **Hampden Bridge**. Motorists wishing to visit the Southern Highlands can continue on from Kangaroo Valley to **Fitzroy Falls** and beyond (*see* Southern Highlands).

To return to Sydney via the scenic South Coast follow the Princes Highway and then the Southern Freeway. The turnoff for Sydney is before Wollongong and from there you continue up to the top of the escarpment then onto the freeway. From the top of **Bulli Pass** the spectacular bird's-eye view of the city of Wollongong fringed by beaches and the ocean is unforgettable. Sydney is only an hour's drive from here back along the freeway.

Useful Information

GETTING THERE
The railway down the **South Coast**
hugs oceanside cliffs and burrows through
mountains that are equally impressive.
Rail travellers can also alight at **Unanderra**
for the connecting steam train up to the
Southern Highlands (*see* previous pages).

Australia's Industrial World: Wollongong; open
every Wed and Fri at 9.30am, tours cost $15;
tel: 4275–7023.
Budderoo National Park: tel: (02) 4423–9800.

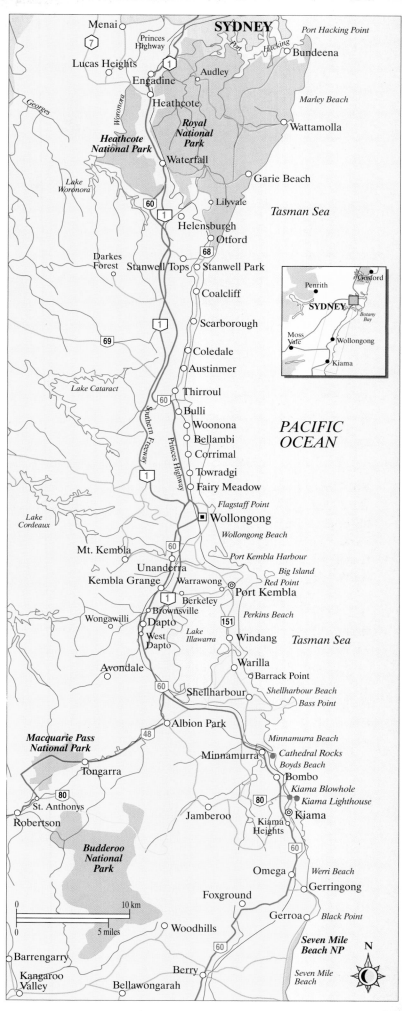

Menai
Princes Highway
7
Lucas Heights
SYDNEY
Port Hacking Point
Port Hacking
Bundeena
Engadine
1
Audley
Heathcote
Marley Beach
Georges
Woronora
Royal National Park
Wattamolla
Heathcote National Park
Waterfall
Lake Woronora
60
Garie Beach
Tasman Sea
1
Lilyvale
Helensburgh
Otford
Darkes Forest
68
Stanwell Tops
Stanwell Park
1
Coalcliff
69
Scarborough
Lake Cataract
Coledale
Austinmer
60
Thirroul
Southern Freeway
Bulli
Woonona
Bellambi
Corrimal
1
Princes Highway
Towradgi
Fairy Meadow
PACIFIC OCEAN
Flagstaff Point
Lake Cordeaux
Wollongong
Wollongong Beach
Mt. Kembla
60
Port Kembla Harbour
Unanderra
Big Island
Kembla Grange
Warrawong
Red Point
Port Kembla
1
Berkeley
Wongawilli
Brownsville
Perkins Beach
Dapto
151
West Dapto
Lake Illawarra
Windang
Tasman Sea
Avondale
Warilla
Barrack Point
60
Shellharbour
Shellharbour Beach
Bass Point
Albion Park
48
Macquarie Pass National Park
Minnamurra Beach
Minnamurra
Cathedral Rocks
Tongarra
Boyds Beach
Bombo
Kiama Blowhole
80
80
Kiama Lighthouse
St. Anthonys
Jamberoo
Kiama
Robertson
Kiama Heights
Budderoo National Park
60
Omega
Werri Beach
Foxground
Gerringong
0   10 km
0   5 miles
Gerroa
Black Point
Woodhills
Seven Mile Beach NP
Barrengarry
Berry
Seven Mile Beach
Kangaroo Valley
Bellawongarah
N

Inset map: Penrith · Gosford · SYDNEY · Botany Bay · Moss Vale · Wollongong · Kiama

Directories

SHOPPING

Antiques

Queen Street, Woollahra (*see* Day 4), is Sydney's antique centre. Look for antique jewellery at **Anne Schofield Antiques**, 36 Queen Street, tel: 9363–1236; furniture, porcelain and metals at **G.L. Auchinachie & Son Antiques**, 43 Queen Street, tel: 9363–4033; decorative arts at **Copeland & De Soos**, 66 Queen Street, tel: 9363–5388; Australian antique prints and maps at **Tony Ward's Printique**, 82 Queen Street, tel: 9363–1422. **Woollahra Antiques Centre**, 160 Oxford Street, tel: 9327–8840, hosts over 50 antique dealers.

Art

Paddington (*see* Day 4) boasts the largest concentration of galleries in Australia. For Aboriginal art the best places are **Co-ee Aboriginal Art**, 98 Oxford Street, tel: 9332–1544; **Caspian Gallery**, 469 Oxford Street, tel: 9331–4260; **Hogarth Galleries**, 7 Walker Lane (opposite 6a Liverpool Street), tel: 9360–6839; and the **Aboriginal & Tribal Art Centre**, 117 George Street, tel: 9247–9625.

Works by Australian masters and contemporary artists are exhibited by many Paddington galleries including **Australian Galleries**, 15 Roylston Street, tel: 9360–5177; **Barry Stern Galleries**, 19–21 Glenmore Road, tel: 9331–4676; **Olsen Carr**, 76 Paddington Street, tel: 9360–9854; and **Josef Lebovic Gallery**, 34 Paddington Street, tel: 9332–1840. Further afield is **Ray Hughes Gallery**, 270 Devonshire Street, Surrey Hills, tel: 9698–3200, good for contemporary works; and **The Ken Done Gallery**, 1–5 Hickson Road, The Rocks, tel: 9247–2740, devoted to this artist's colourful works.

For books on Australian art the **Gallery Shop at the Art Gallery of NSW** (*see* Day 2), tel: 9225–1744, has Australia's most comprehensive collection.

Books

For Australian authors like Nobel Prize-winner Patrick White and Thomas Keneally of *Schindler's List* fame, and for a large selection of books on Australia, head for the city's biggest bookshops like **Angus & Robertson**, Imperial Arcade, 174–186 Pitt Street, tel: 9235–1188; or **Dymocks**, 428 George Street, tel: 9235–0155.

Bookshops with atmosphere include **Gleebooks** (*see* Day 3), 49 Glebe Point Road, Glebe, tel: 9660–2333, with Sunday afternoon readings; and **Berkelouw** antiquarian books and its coffee shop, 19 Oxford Street, Paddington, tel: 9360–3200; this store also runs a barn-like country outlet at Berrima (*see* Southern Highlands).

Clothing

The elegant 19th-century **Strand Arcade** (*see* Day 2), 412 George Street, hosts top Aussie designers like Edmiston, who dresses Nicole Kidman and other stars, at Shop 68, tel: 9380–8787; visit **Coogi**, ground floor, for colourful Melbourne-designed handknits; and **Strand Hatters**, Shop 8, tel: 9231–6884, for Aussie-style Akubra hats.

At the **Queen Victoria Building** (*see* Day 2) look for **Country Road**, 2 Grand Walk, for stylish Australian clothing; **Done Art & Design**, which is also in The Rocks; and **Purely Australian**, level 2, which stocks R.M. Williams' country-style clothes and Driza-Bone all-weather coats.

For inspired original Aussie surfwear check out **Hot Tuna**, 180 Oxford Street, Paddington; and **Mambo**, next to the Verona Cinema, also on Oxford Street.

Well-known international designer boutiques like **Moschino**, **Chanel**, **Christian Lacroix**, and **Louis Vuitton** are centred on King Street, while **Emporio Armani** and its cafe are at Challis House, 4 Martin Place. **Polo Ralph Lauren** is in the Queen Victoria Building, as are **Guess**, **Esprit** and **Pierre Cardin**.

Department Stores

Sydney's most famous department store is **David Jones** (*see* Day 2) on Elizabeth Street, the original store where women's wear is predominant. The men's wear and homeware building is opposite on Market Street. Both stores are excellent for fine fashion, quality shoes, leather goods, make-up and toiletries as well as a variety of homeware, while downstairs on Market Street is the fabulous food hall.

On the Pitt Street Mall is **Grace Bros**, who, along with **David Jones**, usually have outlets in all the major shopping malls around the Greater Sydney area.

Duty Free

Downtown Duty Free are at 105 Pitt Street and Lower Ground Floor in the Strand Arcade, as well as at the Sydney International Airport.

Gems and Jewellery

Find Australia's renowned opals at **Percy Marks**, 60–70 Elizabeth Street, tel: 9233–1355; **The Rocks Opal Mine**, Clocktower Square, The Rocks, tel: 9247–4974; **Flame Opals**, 119 George Street; and **Black Ridge Opal Mine**, Darling Harbour. For unique pink Argyle diamonds go to **The House of Giulians**, cnr of George and Bridge streets, tel: 9252–2051; the **Perth Mint**, Heritage Building, cnr of York and Druitt streets, tel: 9267–7481; and Cellinis, Shop 31, Gallery Level, Centrepoint. For world-class Broome pearls, head for **Paspaley Pearls**, 142 King Street, tel: 9232–7633.

Markets

Colourful, bustling and the place to find bargains, bric-a-brac and handicrafts, the city's best-known markets are held every weekend.

Paddington Market (*see* Day 4), Village Church, 395 Oxford Street, tel: 9331–2646, is held on Saturdays 10am–5pm, and is good for original clothing, jewellery, art, handicrafts and bric-a-brac. **The Rocks Market** (*see* Day 1), George Street North, tel: 9255–1717, is held on Saturdays and Sundays 10am–5pm and is great for homeware and antiques. **The Balmain Market** (*see* Day 6), St Andrew's Church, Darling Street, tel: 9818–2674, is held on Saturdays 8am–4pm, and has an unusual selection of handmade gifts and crafts.

ABOVE *Bright bags, colourful clothes, special souvenirs, sumptuous snacks, marvellous musicians and friendly faces are all at the Paddington market.*

TOP *These colourful crafts and a great variety of interesting bric-a-brac are to be found at Sydney's various markets.*

OPPOSITE TOP *In the city's shadow, The Rocks provides a great setting for picking up a bargain at the weekend market.*

Malls

Take a 'mall crawl' through some of Sydney's largest shopping centres. The best in the city is **Pitt Street Mall**, a pedestrian thoroughfare that is lined with speciality stores, arcades and shopping complexes including the six-level **Skygarden**; **Centrepoint**, a maze of fashion boutiques; and **Glasshouse**, a three-level shopping centre.

Photography

Head for the excellent **Byron Mapp Gallery** for Australian and international photography exhibitions and books on photography and cinema. The Gallery is located at 178 Oxford Street, Paddington, tel: 9331–2929, and has its own on-site cafe. For photographic supplies **Fletchers Fotographics**, at 317 Pitt Street, tel: 9267–6146, and **Paxtons**, at 285 George Street, tel: 9299–2999, are comprehensive with duty-free prices.

Souvenirs

Clocktower Square, located in The Rocks, is unashamedly tourist-oriented with a wide range of shops that stock leather goods, koala and wombat soft toys, Australian-theme T-shirts, replica Aboriginal arts and crafts, opals and numerous other gift options. **Harbourside** at Darling Harbour, a popular souvenir centre crammed with Australiana, has over 200 speciality shops. The **Queen Victoria Building** is another option for souvenir-hunting tourists as it has shops offering a variety of upmarket souvenirs on its top level – clothes, gifts and opals. For overall shopping as well as for architectural splendour, nothing can compare with this 19th-century version of the shopping mall.

Shopping

CUISINE

*S*ydney's thriving multicultural eating scene makes dining out in the city a treat. There is a diverse spectrum of ethnic food as well as the exciting Modern Australian cuisine which is emerging from all these cosmopolitan influences. Combined with Sydney's marvellous fresh produce, the choice of where to eat is growing at an astonishing rate. For travellers who enjoy walking along the street to choose a restaurant, the best areas include **Oxford Street** from Darlinghurst to Paddington (*see* Day 4), beachside **Campbell Parade** at Bondi Beach (*see* Day 4), **King Street**, Newtown, and **Glebe Point Road** in Glebe (*see* Day 3) which boasts more restaurants and cafes than any other single city street.

Seafood

The city's freshest seafood is at **The Fish Markets** (*see* Day 3) overlooking Blackwattle Bay at Pyrmont. The seafood array is staggering. Buy take-away fish and chips, or barbecued octopus, a contemporary favourite. You can eat at outdoor waterfront tables. Try raw fish sashimi and sushi at the Japanese restaurant or dine at Doyles, one of four famous seafood restaurants run by the family who started off at Fisherman's Wharf at Watsons Bay (*see* Day 4). **Doyles on the Beach**, tel: 9337–2007, is still the venue of their original and best waterfront restaurant and is renowned for its signature jumbo prawns. Sitting by the dinghies on the beach and watching the sun go down over a panoramic harbour vista is a treat. **Doyles at the Quay** tel: 9252–3400, in the Overseas Passenger Terminal at Circular Quay is also excellent. **Jordans**, on the waterfront at Darling Harbour, tel: 9281–3711, (*see* Day 3) offers elegant seafood dining with enormous platters on the menu. **Waterfront** in Campbells Cove at The Rocks, tel: 9247–3666, (*see* Day 1) offers an

historic waterside setting, while **Sails Harbourside Restaurant** at McMahons Point ferry wharf, tel: 9955–5793, (*see* Day 6) overlooks the Harbour Bridge and the city. **Rimini Fish Café** beside Manly Beach at 35 South Steyne, tel: 9977–3880, (*see* Day 5) offers a great blackboard menu perfect after a bracing ferry trip. Further north, overlooking Whale Beach, is **Jonah's** at 69 Bynya Road, Palm Beach, tel: 9974–5599, the favoured luncheon retreat of the rich and famous (*see* Day 5).

Contemporary Australian

The Rockpool at 107 George Street, The Rocks, tel: 9252–1888, is run by the entrepreneurial Neil Perry with his penchant for Asian ingredients. Nearby **Quay** at the Overseas Passenger Terminal at Circular Quay West tel: 9251–5600, has excellent cuisine and views. At the Opera House, **The Bennelong**'s superb food is matched by the views and fabulous architecture, tel: 9250–7578. **Banc** at 53 Martin Place, tel: 9233–5300, is generally recognised as one of Sydney's top restaurants, and the Hotel Intercontinental's **Treasury Restaurant** is notable for its historic rooms, at 117 Macquarie Street, tel: 9230–0200. Idyllic surrounds, food and service are available at **The Botanic Gardens** restaurant near the duck pond in the gardens, tel: 9241–2419. **Omnivore** at 33 Darling Street, Balmain, tel: 9810–2041 (*see* Day 6), serves breakfast through to dinner. On the corner of Campbell Parade and Hall Street at Bondi Beach, tel: 9365–4422, i **Ravesi's** (*see* Day 4), which has a Mediterranean atmosphere and wonderful beach views from the balcony. In the Blue Mountains (*see* Day 7) enjoy mountain panoramas from **Lilians** at Lilianfels Avenue, Katoomba, tel: 4780–1200, and five-star cuisine at **Cleopatra's**, an historic guest house at 118 Cleopatra Street, Blackheath, tel: 4787–8456. In the Hunter Valley (*see* Hunter Valley) it is hard to go past **Roberts** at Peppertree, on Halls Road, tel: 4998–7330; **Chez Pok** at Peppers Guest house; or **Blaxland's** on Broke Road, tel: 4998–7550. At Bowral in the Southern Highlands (*see* Southern Highlands), splurge in the country-house splendour of **Milton Park**, Horderns Road, Bowral, tel: 4861–1522.

Best Cafes

Bar Coluzzi, at 322 Victoria Street, Darlinghurst, tel: 9380–5420, provides the blueprint for Sydney's cafe culture. **La Mensa**, next door to the Australian Centre for Photography at 257 Oxford Street, tel: 9332–2963, offers chic cafeteria dining and Paddington Street views, as does the **Verona Cafe** on Oxford Street beside the Verona Cinema, tel: 9360–3226 (*see* Day 4). At the **MCA Cafe** at the Museum of Contemporary Art in Circular Quay, tel: 9241–4253 (*see* Day 1), the food is as

avant garde as the exhibits, with fabulous views to match. **Café Sydney**, on the fifth floor of Customs House (*see* Day 1), offers indoor and outdoor dining with spectacular views of Sydney Harbour, while **Quay Bar**, designed to reflect Sydney bars of old, has an oyster bar and outdoor piazza dining. **Harris Coffee and Tea** in the Strand Arcade (*see* Day 2) serves traditional morning and afternoon teas. At **The Barracks Cafe** at the Hyde Park Barracks in Queens Square, tel: 9223–8922 (*see* Day 2), stop for sunny courtyard lunches, and at the Art Gallery of NSW (*see* Day 2) stop off at the **Gallery Cafe** for coffee and cakes and great views of Wolloomooloo Bay. In the east, **Cosmo Terrace Cafe** on Knox Street, Double Bay, tel: 9326–2928 (*see* Day 4), is great for society voyeurs, while at Avalon on the northern beaches, enjoy coffee and cakes while browsing the book-shelves at the popular **Bookocinno**, 37a Old Barrenjoey Road, Avalon, tel: 9973–1244 (*see* Day 5). Vegetarian snacks and herbal teas are good at **Cranks Cafe** by the ferry wharf at Parramatta, tel: 9891–3662 (*see* Day 6). Visitors to the Blue Mountains (*see* Day 7) are lured by Leura's cafes along The Mall including **Landseers** at No. 178 and **Leura Gourmet** at No. 159. The must-visit cafe in the mountains is the heritage-listed

ABOVE *Excellent fresh produce is on offer at the various Sydney markets.*

TOP *Doyles seafood restaurant at the Quay is the latest of their four fabulous and famous venues.*

OPPOSITE *Fishmongers at the Sydney Fish Markets pack the fresh catch in ice for delivery all around the state.*

Paragon at 65 Katoomba Street, Katoomba, tel: 4782–2928, with its original Art Deco interior, old-fashioned fare and excellent handmade chocolates. On the Central Coast, stop at the **Haven Beach Cafe** at Haven Beach, Terrigal, tel: 4385–2061, for waterfront dining (*see* Central Coast).

Asian Cuisines

Chinta Ria Temple of Love at Cockle Bay (*see* Day 3), tel 9264–3211 offers delicious Malaysian Hawker-style food, live jazz (on Tuesdays), and a temple-like décor with a giant Buddha in the centre. **Sailors Thai Canteen**, in the heritage-listed Sailors Home at 106 George Street, The Rocks, tel: 9251–2466, is good for lunch (*see* Day 1). Wander down

King Street, Newtown for more Thai restaurants.

Chinese establishments thrive in Chinatown (*see* Day 3) and for a fascinating food experience try yum cha at **Silver Spring**, Sydney Central Building, 191 Hay Street, tel: 9211–2232.

Malaysian cuisine is best at **Bangkok and Penang Curry Laksa House**, Plaza Food Court, Dixon Street in Chinatown, tel: 9281–2737, which offers a variety of cheap Asian food. **The Laksa House** in The Greenwood Tree Hotel, 182 Oxford Street, Paddington, tel: 9360–6401, is also popular (*see* Day 4).

Japanese cuisine with great views is at its best at **Unkai** in the ANA Hotel, 176 Cumberland Street, The Rocks, tel: 9250–6123.

Award-winning Indian is at **Flavour of India**, 120–128 New South Head Road, Edgecliff, tel: 9326–2659 (*see* Day 4), and its sister shop at 142a Glebe Point Road, Glebe, tel: 9692–0662.

Vietnamese cuisine is best at **Cabramatta** in the far-western suburbs and for Asian gourmands is well worth the 45-minute train ride. Closer to town is **Old Saigon** at 107 King Street, Newtown, tel: 9519–5931. Modern Asian is unsurpassed at the classy **Wockpool** at the Southern Proemade, Darling Harbour, tel: 9211-9888.

Mediterranean

Flavours blend at the elegant **Criterion** in the MLC Centre, cnr King and Castlereagh streets, tel: 9233–1234, which specialises in Lebanese, Turkish and Moroccan cuisines (*see* Day 2). **The Edge** (tel: 9360–1372) at 60 Riley Street, East Sydney, serves modern Mediterranean, while **La Bora Ristorante** at 9a Barrack Street, tel: 9233–5296, serves traditional Italian cuisine which is also found at Norton Street, in the inner-west suburb of Leichhardt known as 'Little Italy'. For excellent Lebanese food head for **Habibi Michael**, 147 Oxford Street, Darlinghurst, tel: 9361–5527, where the atmosphere is enlivened by erotic belly dancing.

Cuisine

NIGHTLIFE

Kings Cross has been the nightlife centre of Sydney for decades, offering cabarets, nightclubs, drag queens, street people, porn shops, and adult cinemas as well as numerous dining establishments and cafes. In neighbouring Darlinghurst, especially along **Oxford Street** and **Taylor Square**, there are many upmarket pubs, bars and restaurants which stay open until late.

The best way to find out what's happening after dark in Sydney is to check out the *Metro* liftout in the Friday *Sydney Morning Herald*, which has a comprehensive overview of the following week in cinema, entertainment and exhibitions. The *Daily Telegraph Mirror* also publishes an extensive gig guide on Thursday.

Ask at your hotel for information on '**Night Tours**' which visits pubs at **The Rocks**, a **Kings Cross cabaret**, the **Hard Rock Cafe**, and finally finishes at the **Casino**. For a look at 'middle-Australia's' favourite late-night venues – the services and sporting clubs which boast poker machines, gambling games like Keno, restaurants and big entertainment acts – go for a night out at one of the big rugby-league clubs like **Parramatta Leagues Club** (*see* Day 6), where visitors are always welcome. An overview of the best of Sydney's nightlife venues follows:

Best Bars

Paddington's trendy **Verona Cafe Bar**, upstairs at 17 Oxford Street, tel: 9360–3266, is next door to the cinema of the same name. It is perfect for after-movie drinks and snacks and is open until midnight all week (*see* Day 4). **Jackson's on George**, at 176 George Street in the city, tel: 9247–2727, has 4 floors of bars and entertainment, including a floor dedicated to pool players and a late-night dance club. The **CBD Hotel**, cnr King and Clarence streets, hosts the popular **CBD Bar** with a games room on level 3. The **Dendy Bar and Bistro**, MLC Centre, Martin Place (*see* Day 2), serves drinks with cinematic names inspired by the adjacent movie house and is open all week until late.

Authentic Pubs

The Rocks hosts some of the city's oldest and most original drinking establishments. Sydney's oldest pub, **The Lord Nelson**, 19 Kent Street, The Rocks, has an open fire and dartboard while the **Australian Hotel**, 100 Cumberland Street, specialises in dark beers and traditional entertainment like chess, draughts, and backgammon. In the eastern suburbs the **Lord Dudley**, 236 Jersey Road, Woollahra, has an open fire and English ambience, while the **Rose and Crown**, 9 Glenmore Road, Paddington, offers a similar atmosphere. In the inner west try the **London Hotel**, 234 Darling Street, Balmain, and the **Nag's Head**, 162 St Johns Road, Glebe.

Jazz

The best of Australian and international jazz is always happening at **The Basement** at Circular Quay, while at the historic 19th-century **Marble Bar**, which was moved intact to the basement of the **Hilton Hotel**, 259 Pitt Street, you can listen to jazz and occasional big bands. **The Side On Cafe**, 83 Parramatta Road, Annandale, is a small intimate venue that offers cutting-edge live jazz.

Rock 'n' Roll

Many of Sydney's legendary rock bands like **Midnight Oil** and **INXS** began their careers playing around the big suburban pubs. Check the newspapers for details of what's happening around town. Rock bands play at innercity suburban pubs like the '**Cat and Fiddle**', Darling Street, Balmain; the **Hopetoun**, Foveaux St, Surry Hills, the **Landsdown**, City Road, Broadway; and in the city, the **Metro** on George Street. In the bustling nightlife centre of Kings Cross, **Round Midnight** hosts live bands as does **Selinas**, further east at the **Coogee Bay Hotel** on Coogee Beach.

Opera

With the world's finest contemporary **Opera House**, Sydney's opera season is exciting, chic and first-class. Operas are staged (check newspapers for details) at the Opera Theatre.

Classical

The **Sydney Symphony Orchestra**, the **Australian Chamber Orchestra** and international orchestras and other musical groups perform at the **Opera House** Concert Hall and several venues around the city, including the **Sydney Town Hall**.

Ballet

The **Australian Ballet**, renowned for its world-class performances, dances at the **Sydney Opera House**. Equally well known is the **Sydney Dance Company**. Touring international companies also play at the Opera House or other venues throughout the city.

Theatre

Australian productions are regularly staged at the **Sydney Opera House's Drama Theatre** and Playhouse, the **Wharf Theatre**, Millers Point, **Belvoir Street Theatre**, Surry Hills and the **Ensemble Theatre**, north of the bridge in Kirribilli. You can also catch the large popular musicals at the **Theatre Royal** in King Street, the **Capitol Theatre** at Haymarket, and the **Lyric Theatre** at Star City Casino. During summer, Shakespeare is performed in **The Royal Botanic Gardens**.

ABOVE *The El Alamein Fountain, at the hub of Kings Cross, lights up at night like an exploding golden dandelion.*

OPPOSITE *The atmosphere of Kings Cross, Sydney's Greenwich Village, is reflected in the lights of its shops, cafes and less salubrious attractions.*

BELOW *The Sydney Showboat, like a traditional Mississippi paddle steamer, cruises Sydney Harbour with revellers.*

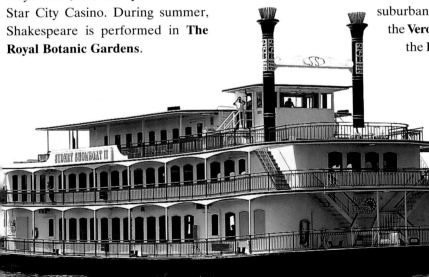

Comedy

The best places to catch up with the latest Australian stand-up comedians are at the popular **Comedy Store**, 450 Parramatta road, Petersham, and the **Comedy Hotel**, 115 Wigram Road, Glebe.

Discos & Nightclubs

Kings Cross and Oxford Street are the areas most densely populated with nightclubs. **Kinselas**, once a funeral parlour, is at 383 Bourke Street, Darlinghurst. **Dancers Cabaret**, at 36 Bayswater Road, Kings Cross, has table-top dancing and hostesses. **Jackson's on George**, 176 George Street in the city, has a dance floor on one of its many levels, while **Home** at the Cockle Bay complex, Darling Harbour (*see* Day 3), has three levels and accommodates up to 2000 people. Head to the **Hard Rock Cafe**, 121-129 Crown Street, or **Planet Hollywood** on George Street to soak up some Americana.

Cinema

Popular blockbusters are shown at the **Hoyts Centre**, **Village** and **Greater Union** complexes on George Street as well as the suburban cinemas. Art Cinema and fringe movies are shown at the **Verona** and the **Chauvel** in Oxford Street, Paddington, and the **Dendy** in Martin Place, and George Street, Newtown.

Casino

Gamblers can walk from Darling Harbour or buses pick up guests from their city hotels to drive them to the **Star City Casino**, a first-class international gaming venue at Pyrmont Bay.

Showboat

Cabaret dinners are a very popular tourist attraction on the wonderful **Sydney Showboat** which leaves Campbell's Cove, The Rocks, tel: 9552–2592, for a harbour cruise with dinner and show.

EVENTS

The best way to find out what's happening is to pick up the free guides at any Visitor Centre or hotel. The *Metro* liftout in Friday's *Sydney Morning Herald* is also very helpful. A brief calendar of events is as follows:

January

Sydney Festival and Carnivale: annual arts and entertainment festival that reflects the city's multicultural character and includes free concerts held at The Domain, tel: 9265–0444.

Adidas International (formerly known as the NSW Open): tennis tournament held at the 'NSW Tennis Centre, Homebush Bay'; tel: 8746–0777.

Australia Day: commemorates the First Fleet landing in Sydney Cove on the 26th January 1788; events include free **Australia Day Concerts** at The Domain, the **Ferrython**, and colourful **Australia Day Events** including fireworks at Darling Harbour.

Chinese New Year: celebrated according to the lunar calendar at Sydney's Chinatown.

February

Hunter Valley Vintage: celebrates grape harvest with activities at the wineries, tel: 4990–4477.

March

Sydney Gay and Lesbian Mardi Gras Festival and Parade: a month-long cultural event (begins in February) which includes film, theatre, cabaret and exhibitions, and culminates in one of the world's most exciting parades at Oxford Street, Paddington.

The Archibald Prize Exhibition: Australia's most prestigious art exhibition at the Art Gallery of NSW, tel: 9225–1700.

Royal Easter Show: the 'country comes to town' with agricultural exhibitions, show-jumping, carnival rides, side-shows, baby animals, cake-decorating, arts and crafts, showbags and a Grand Parade of animals; every Easter at the RAS Showgrounds at Moore Park.

Dragon Boat Festival: held at Cockle Bay in Darling Harbour and attracts over 50 international teams – an annual event in mid-March that has persisted for 15 years.

April

Sydney Autumn Racing Carnival: held during April at the Royal Randwick Racecourse, Randwick, which is only 5 kilometres from Sydney's city centre. Buses leave from

OPPOSITE *Pyrotechnic displays of grand proportions explode off the Sydney Harbour Bridge when the city celebrates New Year's Eve.*

ABOVE *Sydney Harbour comes alive with marine craft from all eras to celebrate Australia Day in January every year.*

Circular Quay and Central Railway Station on Saturdays and public holidays.
Australian Open Swimming Championships: held at the Sydney Aquatic Centre, Homebush, in the last week of April.

May
Sydney Morning Herald **Half Marathon:** held annually, with the circular route starting and ending at the Harbour Bridge.

June
Manly Food and Wine Festival: held at different hotels and restaurants around the Manly area, tel: 9977–1088.

Sydney Film Festival: held at the State Theatre and other selected cinemas for two weeks mid-month, tel: 9660–3844.

July
Yulefest: a dining celebration of Christmas held in the cool winter months in the Blue Mountains when different restaurants and hotels host a Christmas dinner every Saturday night from June through to the end of August.
Sydney International Music Festival: a week-long event held at different venues including the Opera House, Darling Harbour, the Sydney Town Hall, and the Seymour Centre, tel: 9929–5447.

August
***Sun-Herald* City to Surf:** attracts thousands of runners every year for this community street run which begins in the city centre, passes the picturesque eastern harbour suburbs and ends at Bondi Beach, tel: 9635–4974.

September
Spring Racing Carnival: hosted by the Australian Jockey Club and held on the last week of September and the first week of October at the Royal Randwick Racecourse, Randwick – 5 kilometres from the city centre. Bus services leave from Circular Quay and the Central Railway Station on Saturdays and public holidays.
South Pacific Dancesport Championships: a dance spectacular is held in the last week of the month at the NSW State Sport Centre, Homebush, tel: 9626–1200.

October
Manly Jazz Festival: jazz bands play at different Manly Beach venues during the first week of October, tel: 9977–1088.
Blackheath Rhododendron Festival: private and public gardens in Blackheath in the Blue Mountains are open to the public during the colourful rhododendron season during the last week of October and the first week of November, tel: 4787–8695.

November
Bridge to Bridge Water Ski Classic: an annual race held from Brooklyn to Windsor on the Hawkesbury River north of Sydney in November, tel: 9552–4311.
Australian PGA: held during the first week of the month at the NSW Golf Club: the **Greg Norman Classic** is held at the end of the month at The Lakes Golf Club.
Glebe Street Fair: colourful cultural event held in the third week at Glebe Point Road, Glebe, and features arts, music, crafts and cuisine, tel: 9552–1546.

December
Sydney to Hobart Ocean Yacht Race: begins in Sydney Harbour on Boxing Day, 26 December, and finishes in Hobart around 1 January. Spectators jam ferries, pleasure craft and all available harbour viewpoints to watch the start of this world-class event.
New Year's Eve Fireworks: these are launched in a spectacular annual display over the Harbour Bridge and harbour on 31 December to usher in the New Year. Vantage points include Lady Macquarie's Point in the Royal Botanic Gardens.

FAR LEFT *Changing night into day and one year into another, fireworks herald in the New Year in showers of gold over the harbour.*

TOP *Sydney's Gay and Lesbian Mardi Gras is one of Sydney's most colourful events.*

CENTRE *Every year on Boxing Day, competitors in the Sydney to Hobart Ocean Yacht Race pour through the Heads, cheered on by spectators lining the foreshores of the harbour.*

LEFT *Colour blooms at the Blackheath Rhododendron Festival during spring in the Blue Mountains.*

INSET *The smiles say it all: Sydney loves to party and the Australian sense of humour and fun is always on display at the Gay and Lesbian Mardi Gras.*

NDEX

Abbotsford 94
Admiralty House 74, *75*
African Waterhole 118
Afternoon Harbour Cruise
    135, 136
America Bay 85
antiques 164
Anzac Bridge 20, 52, *56*, 57
Anzac War Memorial *38*, 43
Archibald Fountain 30, 38, 39
Argyle Cut 23
Argyle Place 14, 21, 23
art 164
Art Gallery of New South
    Wales 30, *40*, 41, 43
Ashton Park 124, 125
Athol Bay 116
Audley 128, 131
Ausail Yacht Charters 136
Australian Centre for
    Photography 70, 71
Australian Museum of
    Natural History *38*, 39, 43
Australian Walkabout 116
Australia's Industry World
    159, 161
Australia's Last Riverboat
    Postman Cruise 136
Australia's Wonderland
    102, 105, 113
Autumn and Spring Racing
    Carnivals 69
Avalon 834
Avoca Beach 141, 142, *143*

Bald Hill 158
ballet 169
Balloons Aloft 149
Balmain 88, *92*, 96, 97, 99,
    122, 134
Balmain History Trail 88
Balmain Markets 93
Balmain Watch House 88, 99
Balmoral 135
Barn, The 124
barramundi 52
Barrenjoey Head 83
Barrenjoey Road 83, 85
bars 168
Basin, The 85
Bayview 85
Bells Line of Road 102, 112
Belmont 141
Bennelong Restaurant 25

Berowra Waters Settlement 136
Berrima 153, *154*
Berry 158, *160*
Big Marley 129
Big Marley Beach 129
Bilgola Beach 83
Bilpin 112
Birchgrove 92
Birchgrove Park 93
Blacket, Edmund 60
Blackheath 111
Blackwattle Bay *52*
Blaxland 105
Blaxland's 105, 149
Blue Gum Forest 111
Blue Mountains 37, 102–113
Blue Mountains Information
    Centre 110
Bobbin Head *136*
Bondi 60
Bondi Beach 60, *66*
Bondi Golf Course 66
Bookocinno 83, 85
Botanic Gardens Restaurant 26
Bouddi National Park 83, 141, *142*
Bowral 152, *153*, 155
Bradfield Highway 19, 21
Bradleys Head 75, 116, 124, 125
Bradman Museum *153*
Brisbane Water 140
Broken Bay 83
Bronte Beach 69
Brooklyn 136, *137*
Budderoo National Park
    160, 161
Budgewoi 141
Bulli Pass 160
Bundeena 128
Bundeena Coast Walk 128
Bungan Beach 83
Burrawang 155
Buskers End 153

Cadman, John 18
Cadman's Cottage *18*, 27
cafes 166
Cahill's Lookout 111
Camp Cove 64, 65
Campbell Parade 66
Campbells Cove 18, 135
Campbells Storehouse 18
Captain Cook Cruises 135, 136
casino 169
Centennial Park 60, *68*, 69, 71
Central Coast 136, 140–143
Central Railway Station 55, 102

Centrepoint Arcade 37, 43
Cessnock 146
Charles Street Wharf 97, 99
Chatswood 85
Chauvel cinema 71
Chez Pok 149
Chimpanzee Park 118
Chinatown 46, 54, 55, 57
Chinese Garden 46, 54, *55*, 57
Church Point 85
Church Point Charter 136
cinema 169
Circular Quay *14*, 19, 23, 27, 30,
    60, 64, 71, 89, 99, 102, 118,
    119, 122, 125, 134
CityRail 30
Clarkes Point Reserve 94
Cleopatra's 111
Cliff Drive 108
Clifton Gardens 124
Clocktower Square 23
Clontarf 125
Clontarf Beach 122
clothing 164
Clovelly 69
Cockatoo Run 155
Cockle Bay 46, 50
Cockle Bay Promenade 52
Collaroy Beach 83
Concord Bridge 94
Conservatorium of Music 26, 27
Convent Garden Hotel *56*, 57
Convict Experience Tours 39, 43
Coogee Beach 60, *68*, 69
Corso, The 78, 80, *81*
Cosmos Terrace Cafe 61
Cottage Point *84*, 85
Cowan Creek 136
Cox, Phillip 46
Cranks Cafe 97
Crater Cove Lookout 125
Cremorne 75
Cremorne Point *122*
Cruising Yacht Club 60
cuisine 166–167
Cumberland Place 23
Customs House *27*

Dalwood 149
Darling Harbour 20, *46*, 47, 50,
    51, 52, 54, 55, 57, 122,
    134, 135
Darling Point 60, 65, 75
Darling Street 92
Darling Street Wharf 88
Darlinghurst 71

David Jones *37*
Dawes Point Park 21
Dee Why 83
Deer Pool 129, 130, 131
department stores 164
Dobroyd Head 125
Domain, The 41
Dong Seng Souvenir Shop 54
Double Bay 60, 61, 75
Dover Heights 66
Doyles 64
Drummoyne 96, 97
Drummoyne Foreshore
    Walkway 88, 94
Duffys Forest 85, 136
duty free 165

Eastern Creek 102
Echo Point 110
Elizabeth Bay House 43
Elizabeth Farm 88, 96, 97
Elizabeth Semillon 146
Empress Falls 106
Entertainment Centre 55, 57
Entrance, The *141*
Evening Lights Harbour
    Cruise 135, 136
events and festivals 170–173
Everglades Gardens *108*,
    109, 113
Experiment Farm Cottage *98*, 99

Fairfax Heritage Track 111
Fairlight 125
Fairy Bower 80, *81*
Farm Cove 14
Faulconbridge 106
Federal Pass Trail 110
First Farm Exhibition 26
First Fleet 14
First Fleet Park *15*, 23
Fisher Bay 122, 125
Fisherman's Wharf 64
Fitzroy Falls 153, *154*, 160
Flagship Charter 135
Flinders, Matthew 40
Forest Coach Lines 85
Fort Denison 74, 85
Fort Scratchley 142, 143
Forth and Clyde Hotel 93
Forty Baskets Beach 125
Fox Studios 69
Fraser, Dawn 88

Gallery Cafe 41
Gallery Shop 41

Gap, The 60, 64
Garden Island 41
Garie Beach *128*, *129*, *131*
Garigal Aboriginal Heritage
    Walk 85
Gay and Lesbian Mardi Gras
    70, *71*
General Post Office 37
George Street *18*, 23, 37
Gerringong 160
Gerroa 160
Giant Stairway *103*, *110*, 111
Gibson, Mel 18, 135
Gladesville Bridge 88, 92, *94*, 95
Gladesville Wharf 94
Gladstone Park 93
Glebe 46, 57
Glebe Point Road *57*
Glenbrook 105
Gosford 140, 142, *143*
Government House 19, *26*, 27
Govetts Leap Road 111
Grand Canyon 111, *112*, 113
Grand Circular Drive 102
Great North Walk 94
Great Western Highway 102,
    105, 113
Greenway, Francis 26, 38, 39, 113
Greenwich Point 94
Grose River 103
Grose Valley *102*, 103, 105, 113,
    111, 113
Grotto Point 125

Hacking River 131
Hambledon Cottage 98, 99
Hamilton 142
Hampden Bridge 160
Harbour Twilight Cruise 14
Harbourside Festival
    Marketplace 46, *47*, 52, 57
Harnett Park 124
Harris Coffee and Tea 37
Harris Street Motor Museum
    52, 57
Haven Beach Cafe 141
Hawkesbury Museum and
    Tourist Centre 113
Hawkesbury River 85, 136
Hawkesbury River Ferries 136
Hawkesbury Valley 112, 134
Haymarket Station 52
Hazelbrook 106
Heads, The 125
Hen and Chicken Bay 94
Heritage Foreshore Track 60, 61

Hermit Bay 61
Hero of Waterloo 21
Hickson Road 18
HMAS *Bounty* 18, *19*, 135
HMAS *Sydney* Mast 124, *125*
Holidays-A-Float 136
Holy Trinity (Garrison)
    Church 21
Homebush Bay 88, *95*
Honeymoon Lookout 108
Hotel Inter-Continental 27
Hume Highway 152
Hunter Estate 149
Hunter River 142
Hunter Valley 146–149
Hunter Valley Motorcycle
    Tours 149
Hunter Valley Tourism
    Services 146
Hunters Hill 94
Hyde Park 30, 38, *39*
Hyde Park Barracks *39*, 43
Hydro Majestic Hotel 102,
    111, 113

Jamberoo 160
Jamison Valley 102, *104*, 105,
    106, 107, 108, 113
jewellery 165
Jibbon Beach 128
Jibbon Head 128
John Tebbut Observatory 113
Jonahs 83
Jungle Cats 118
Juniper Hall 71
Justice and Police Museum 27,
    39, 43

Kangaloon 155
Kangaroo Valley *152*, 155, 160
Katoomba 102, *108*, 110, 113
Katoomba Falls 110
Kendall, Henry 69
Kiama *158*, *159*
Kim's Beachside Retreat 141
Kincumber 140
Kings Cross 30, 41, 42, 43, 60
Kirribilli 19
Kirribilli House 74
Koala Encounters *116*, 117
Ku-ring-gai Chase National Park
    84, *85*, 136, 140
Kurrajong Heights 112

La Mensa 70
Lady Bay Beach 64

Lady Carrington Drive 131
Lake Illawarra 159
Lake Macquarie 141
Lane Cove River 94, 134
Lapstone 105
Lavender Bay 19, 88, *89*, 94
Lawrence, D.H. 158, 159
Lawson 106
Lawson, Henry 69
Leura 102, 108, 113
Leura Cascades 108
Leura Village Mall 108
Lilians 110
Lindeman's *146*, 147
Linden 106
Lion Island 83
Little Marley 128, 129
Little Marley Beach 129
Little Sirius Cove 75
Loftus 131
London Hotel 93
Long Reef *83*
Lord Howe Island 61
Louisa Road 93
Luna Park *94*, 95

Mackerel Beach 85
MacPherson, Elle 106
Macquarie Lighthouse 66
Macquarie Pass 155
Macquarie Street 30, 38, 39, 43
Macquarie, Lachlan 14
malls 165
Manly 74, *75*, *78*, 85, 122,
    125, 134
Manly Beach *78*, 79
Manly Cove 125
Manly Ferry 125
Manor, The 124
Mariners Church 18, 27
markets 165
Marley Creek 129, 130, 131
Marley Headland 129
Martin Place 30, *37*, 38, 43
Matilda Cruises 135, 136
MCA Cafe 15
McCarrs Creek Road 85
McMahons Point 88, 94
Meadowbank 94, 97
Medlow Bath 111
Megalong Valley 111
Middle Harbour 134, *135*
Middle Head 75
Milsons Point 20, 88, 94
Milton Park 155
Milton Park Hotel *154*, 155

Minnamurra Rainforest 160
Mitchell Wing 40, 41, 43
Mittagong 152
Mona Vale 83, 85
Moore Park 116
Moore Park Golf Course 69
Morning Harbour Cruise
    134, 136
Mort Bay Park 93
Mortlake Ferry 94
Morton National Park 155
Mosman 135
Mosman Bay 75, 122, *123*
Moss Vale 153, 155
Mount Colah 136
Mount Ku-ring-gai 136
Mount Pleasant Winery 146
Mount Tomah Botanic Gardens
    102, 113
Mount Victoria 112
Mount View Road 146
Mount Wilson 112
Mrs Macquarie's Chair 14, 25
Mrs Macquarie's Point 25
Museum of Contemporary Art
    15, 27
Museum of Sydney 14, 27
music 168

Nan Tien Temple *159*
Narrabeen *82*, 83
National Artillery Museum 80, 85
National Maritime Museum
    46, 47, 50, *51*, 57
Newcastle 140, *142*, 143
Norman Lindsay Gallery and
    Museum *106*, 113

Ocean Beach 141
Oceanworld, Manly 78, *79*, 85
Old Government House *98*, 99
Old Sydney Town 140, *141*
Orang-utan Forest 118
Overseas Visitors Passenger
    Terminal *18*
Oxford Street *70*, 71

Paddington Town Hall 71
Palm Beach Experience 85
Park Hyatt 19, *20*, 21
Parramatta 88, 92, 94–97,
    99, 113
Parramatta Explorer 97, 99
Parramatta Park 99
Parramatta River 88, 92, 94,
    96, 97, 134

Index

Parramatta Visitors Centre 99
Pearces Corner 136
Pearl Beach 141
Penrith 105
Peppers *149*
Phillip, Captain Arthur 74, 75
photography 165
Pier One 20
Pitt Street 55
Pitt Street Mall 30, *37*
Pittwater *82, 83,* 134
Pittwater Road 80, 85
Point Piper 61
Pokolbin Estate Vineyard 146
Pokolbin Flora Reserve 146
Pokolbin Horse Coaches 149
Pokolbin Valley 146
Port Hacking 128
Port Jackson 19
Port Kembla *159*
Potts Point 41, 60, 75
Powerhouse Museum 46, *52,* 57
Princes Highway 158, 159, 160
pubs 168
Pulpit Rock 111
Putney Point 94
Pylon Lookout *23,* 27
Pyrmont Bridge *50*

Quayside Booking Centre 134
Queen Street 69
Queen Victoria Building 30, *34,*
  35, 36, 37, 43
Queens Wharf 142, 143
Queenscliff 78

Rainforest Birds 118
Randwick Racecourse 60, *69,* 71
Ravesi's 66
Reef Beach 125
Richmond 102, 112
Richmond RAAF Base 113
Rimini Fish Cafe 80
Rip Bridge 141
Ripples Houseboat Hire 136
RiverCat *88,* 94, *97,* 99
Robertson 154, 155
Robertson Park 64
Robert's at Peppertree 149
Rocks, The 14, 18, 19, 23,
  122, 135
Rocks Square 23, 27
Rocks Visitor Centre 18, 27
Rose Bay 61, 65, 75, 122, 134
Royal Botanic Gardens 14, 19,
  24, 25, 60, 74, 122

Royal National Park 128,
  130, 158
Rushcutters Bay 60, *61,* 75

S.H. Ervin Gallery 23, 27
Sacred Heart Convent 60, 71
Sails Restaurant 94
Sandy Bay 125
Sarah's Walk 124
Scenic Drive, The 141
Scenic Railway 110, 113
seafood 166
Seal Theatre 116, 118
Seaplane Wharf 83
Serpentaria 118
Seven Mile Beach 160
Shark Beach 61
Shark Island 75
Shell Cove 122, *123*
Shelley Beach 78, 80, *81*
Shellharbour 159
shopping 164–167
Skyway 113
Snails Bay 93
Snapperman Beach 85
Solway Lass 135, 136
South Bondi 66
South Coast 158–161
South Head *64,* 65
South Steyne 78, *80*
Southern Highlands
  152–155, 161
Southern Highlands Visitor
  Information Centre 153, 155
souvenirs 165
Spit, The 125
Spit Bridge 122, 125, 135
Sportspace Tours 71
Springwood 106, 107
St Andrew's Cathedral 35, 43
St Andrew's Congregational
  Church 93
St Ives 85, 136
St James' Church 38
St Mark's Anglican Church
  60, 71
St Mary's Cathedral 30, *39,* 43
St Matthew's Anglican
  Church 113
St Patrick's Cemetery 99
St Patrick's College 80
Stanwell Park 158, *160, 161*
Star City Casino 46, 57
State Library of New South
  Wales *40, 41,* 43
State Parliament House 40

State Sports Centre 97
State Theatre 30, 37, 43
Station Beach 83
Strand Arcade 37
Strathfield 102
Sublime Point Lookout 108
Suez Canal 23
surfing 66, 69
Surveyor General Inn 153
Susannah Place 23, 27
Swansea 141
Sydney Aquarium 46, 47, *50,* 57
Sydney Buses Ticket Kiosk 60
Sydney By Sail 135, 136
Sydney Cove 14, 19, 21
Sydney Cricket Ground 60,
  69, 71
Sydney Explorer Bus 27, 43, 60,
  61, 66, 69
Sydney Fish Markets 46, *52,* 57
Sydney Football Stadium 69
Sydney Harbour Bridge 14, 15,
  19, 21, 25, 27, 94, 122
Sydney Harbour Explorer
  134, 135
Sydney Harbour National Park
  75, 80, 124, 125
Sydney Heads 135
Sydney Mint Museum 39, 43
Sydney Observatory 14, 23
Sydney Olympic Park 88, 99, 135
Sydney Opera House 22, *25,*
  74, 135
Sydney Rowing Club 94
Sydney Seafood School 52, 57
Sydney to Hobart Ocean Yacht
  Race 64
Sydney Tower 30, 37, 47, 57
Sydney Town Hall 30, *31,* 43
Sydney Tropical Centre *26,* 27
Sydney University 46, 57

Tall-Ship Sailing Tours 135
Tamarama Bay 66
Taronga Zoo 75, 116–119,
  134, 135
Tasman Sea 142
Tasmanian Devil 116
Taylor Square 60, 71
Taylors Bay 124
Terrigal *140,* 141
Terry Hills 85
theatre 169
Thirroul 159
Three Sisters 102, 103, 108,
  110, 113

Toowoon Bay 141
Toronto 141
Town Hall Station 30
Treasury Building 27
Tried and Transported Tour
  39, 43
Tuggerah Lake 141
Tulip Festival *153*
Tyrrells 146

Unanderra 155, 161
Utzon, Jørn 25
Vagabond Cruises 136
Valentia Street Wharf 94
Valley Heights 105
Valley of the Waters Reserve
  106, *107,* 113
Vaucluse House 60, 61, 71
Venture Cruises 136
Victoria Barracks 71

Walsh Bay 88
Waratah Park 85
Warners Bay 141
Warrimoo 105
Warringah Mall 80, 85
Waterman's Cottage 88, 92, 99
Waterrun 128
Watsons Bay 60, 61, 64, *65,*
  75, 135
Watsons Bay Park 66
Waverley Cemetery *69,* 71
Wentworth Falls 102, 108,
  109, 113
Wentworth, William Charles
  61, 64
West Head Road 85
Western Motorway 102
Whale Beach 83
Wharf Theatre 20
White, Patrick 112
Wildes Meadow 155
William Street 42, 43
Windmill Hill 23
Windsor 102, 113
Wollongong 158, 159, 160, 161
Woolahra 69, 71
Woolloomooloo *41,* 60, 75
Writers Walk 23
Wylie's Baths 69
Wyndham Estate 149

Yestergrange 108, 113
Yurulbin 88
Yurulbin Park 92, 93
Yurulbin Point 94

Index